LIFE ALONG THE WAY SERIES
BY JOURNEY**WISE**

A 90-DAY DEVOTIONAL

# JESUS WITH US

## MEETING HIM WHERE HE BEGAN

WHITAKER
HOUSE

*Note:* This book is not intended to provide medical or psychological advice or to take the place of medical advice and treatment from your personal physician. Those who are having suicidal thoughts or who have been emotionally, physically, or sexually abused should seek help from a mental health professional or qualified counselor. Neither the publisher nor the author nor the author's ministry or business takes any responsibility for any possible consequences from any action taken by any person reading or following the information in this book. If readers are taking prescription medications, they should consult with their physicians and not take themselves off prescribed medicines without the proper supervision of a physician. Always consult your physician or other qualified health care professional before undertaking any change in your physical regimen, whether fasting, diet, medications, or exercise.

**JESUS WITH US:**
*Meeting Him Where He Began*

JourneyWise
PO Box 382662
Germantown, TN 38183
https://journeywise.network/

ISBN: 979-8-88769-058-2
eBook ISBN: 979-8-88769-059-9
Printed in the United States of America
© 2023 by The Moore-West Center for Disciple Formation

Whitaker House
1030 Hunt Valley Circle
New Kensington, PA 15068
www.whitakerhouse.com

Library of Congress Cataloging-in-Publication data has been applied for.

1 2 3 4 5 6 7 8 9 10 11 ⨆⨆ 30 29 28 27 26 25 24 23

# CONTENTS

# FOREWORD

His arrival astonished our human expectations. Matthew describes it in this way: "'They will call him Immanuel' (which means 'God with us')" (Matthew 1:23).

God came to earth in Jesus Christ to be with us. We have the privilege of traveling through life with the greatest Teacher, Friend, and Savior we could ever know.

Where are you in your journey with Jesus? As with any trip, to arrive at your desired destination, you must first begin. Therefore, each leg of a journey starts with the first step. If you want to finish well, it matters where you begin. That is why, in this first devotional of the Life Along the Way Series, *Jesus with Us*, we must meet Jesus where He began.

Scripture is clear that Jesus Himself had no "beginning." He is the eternal God—God the Son—from everlasting to everlasting. (See John 1.) But Jesus left His throne in glory, robed Himself in humanity, and intersected our lives. Therefore, to walk with Jesus through His earthly existence is to witness a holy God enter into humanity's journey and make it His own in order to redeem us and give us true life.

As we join Jesus on His journey, we stop at important early places along the path: the stories of Jesus's earthly mother and father, Mary and Joseph; Jesus's humble birth in Bethlehem; the fulfillment of the promises of His coming; His being protected from a plot to kill Him as a child; His longing for His heavenly Father as a youth; the calling of His first followers; the start of His ministry to announce the arrival of the kingdom of heaven; and His life-transforming Sermon on the Mount.

The beginning of Jesus's story is powerful, but I believe you will also find it personal. As you read this devotional, I encourage you to reflect in a personal way on the beginning of Jesus's earthly life. For example, if you are a parent, how would you feel if you were Mary or Joseph? As a member of a family, what do you notice about the relationships you see in Jesus's family? If you are invested in a career, what were the important principles that guided you when you began your own work? I believe you will discover familiar sites and emotions. Embrace them. I pray that by doing so, you will find yourself walking ever more closely with the One who is with you always.

—*Shane Stanford*
Founder and CEO, The Moore-West Center for Applied Theology
President, JourneyWise

# WELCOME TO LIFE ALONG THE WAY

From the moment we take our first breath, life is a journey. We experience growth, disappointment, difficulty, pain, love, blessing, happiness, struggle, hope, and aging. All of these experiences, in their own unique way, shape us and create the story of our lives.

So, why is it that so many of us focus on escaping this life? Some of us approach life on earth as merely a stop along the way to our eternal destination. Others of us spend far more time worrying about the act of dying or fretting over the difficulties of this life than we spend considering whether or not we are living life to its fullest in the here and now and showing love to other people.

More than two thousand years ago, a Man named Jesus also journeyed through life. He experienced everything that we experience, but He had a special mission, and His experience of reaching His destination was a bit different from ours. After He died, He conquered death and rose again, entering into a brand-new life—one that He offers to us too. He secured the answers to both life and death.

By conquering death, Jesus reached His destination in a new way. He created a path of peace, hope, and meaning for all of us to follow. While Jesus lived with His unique destination in mind, He also was incredibly intentional about the journey. He knew that today shapes tomorrow. And without learning and growing from today, we cannot expect to be ready for tomorrow.

As Christians, we believe that Jesus is alive and working even now. But, what's more, we believe that He is ready and willing to journey *with* us. Did you catch that? Jesus wants to journey with you—yes, you!—in what we here at JourneyWise refer to as "Life Along the Way."

You read that right. Jesus wants to ride shotgun as you navigate your life's path. He wants to help you learn, grow, see, feel, and experience life in a completely new way. He laid all of this out for you and me in the four Gospels: Matthew, Mark, Luke, and John.

We created the four Life Along the Way daily devotionals to capture the essence of Jesus's life, ministry, death, and ascension. And you are holding in your hands book one. (While we encourage you to read the books sequentially, you may read them in any order you choose.)

Each devotional is designed to be read in ninety days, but you can just as easily go at your own pace. It's okay if you get behind or if you read ahead. It's okay if it takes you a year to go through each book. The idea is that you're getting to know the journey of Jesus and allowing His journey to shape and direct yours.

The four Life Along the Way books are as follows:

1. *Jesus with Us: Meeting Him Where He Began*

2. *Jesus Among Us: Walking with Him in His Ministry and Miracles*

3. *Jesus Through Us: Following His Example in Love and Service*

4. *Jesus in Us: Living Wholeheartedly the Life He Intends*

Whether you've been in the church your whole life, are a curious skeptic, or find yourself somewhere in between, we hope that this journey through Scripture focused on the way Jesus "did life" will add great purpose to your *Life Along the Way*. We trust that God will give you wisdom for the journey as He grows you into His likeness and that you will be transformed as you live daily with Jesus.

Philippians 1:6 says, "*I am certain that God, who began the good work within you, will continue his work until it is finally finished on the day when Christ Jesus returns*" (NLT).

As you journey with Jesus, our hope is that you would *love Jesus and love like Jesus.*

It's time to hit the road!

—*The JourneyWise Team*

# DAY 1:
## EVERY JOURNEY BEGINS WITH A STEP

## SCRIPTURE READING

LUKE 1:1–4 (NLT)

*Many people have set out to write accounts about the events that have been ful-filled among us. They used the eyewitness reports circulating among us from the early disciples. Having carefully investigated everything from the beginning, I also have decided to write an accurate account for you, most honorable Theophilus, so you can be certain of the truth of everything you were taught.*

## LIFE LESSONS

Every journey begins with a first step and an acknowledgment that we have many steps yet to take. We must accept that some moments may be hard, while others will seem effortless. Keep in mind that the journey you're under-taking as you read Jesus's story is not a race to the end. Allow yourself to relax and breathe. This trek is designed to provide space for change and reflection, both of which take time.

In compiling his gospel, Luke sought the truth above everything else, and we are following his lead. The stories and teachings of Christ that we'll encounter on our journey come with both loving assurance and a slight reprimand or two to help us get back on track. Either way, they are meant to encourage us to live our best lives, resting in God's love and Christ's hope. Jesus came to bring hope and truth to our lives, and it's important that we never forget that as the days pass. Rest in the truth of Christ's words and take comfort, as you go along, in His promise of hope for a broken world.

We will be taking a chronological look at the life of Jesus through the Gospels, sitting in the shade of His vibrant humanity as He experiences the world around Him.

We hope Christ's life will inspire you, teach you things about yourself and the world around you, and help you feel loved and accepted by God.

## WHERE ARE YOU?

*Have you been on a long journey before? If so, where did you go, and what did you take with you?*

_____

_____

_____

_____

_____

*What did you enjoy about your journey? What is the most memorable part?*

_____

_____

_____

_____

_____

*If you have never been on a long journey, where would you like to travel? Why did you choose that destination?*

_____

_____

_____

_____

_____

## A PRAYER

Jesus, thank You for the messengers who wrote down the gospel accounts of Your life so we can still learn from Your words and teachings today. I pray that this journey will open my eyes to who You are, and that I will learn how to love You and love like You. Give me an open heart and mind as I learn about You. In Your name, amen.

# DAY 2:
## THE UNEXPECTED BLESSING

## SCRIPTURE READING

LUKE 1:5–25 (NLT)

*When Herod was king of Judea, there was a Jewish priest named Zechariah. He was a member of the priestly order of Abijah, and his wife, Elizabeth, was also from the priestly line of Aaron. Zechariah and Elizabeth were righteous in God's eyes, careful to obey all of the Lord's commandments and regulations. They had no children because Elizabeth was unable to conceive, and they were both very old.*

*One day Zechariah was serving God in the Temple, for his order was on duty that week. As was the custom of the priests, he was chosen by lot to enter the sanctuary of the Lord and burn incense. While the incense was being burned, a great crowd stood outside, praying.*

*While Zechariah was in the sanctuary, an angel of the Lord appeared to him, standing to the right of the incense altar. Zechariah was shaken and overwhelmed with fear when he saw him. But the angel said, "Don't be afraid, Zechariah! God has heard your prayer. Your wife, Elizabeth, will give you a son, and you are to name him John. You will have great joy and gladness, and many will rejoice at his birth, for he will be great in the eyes of the Lord. He must never touch wine or other alcoholic drinks. He will be filled with the Holy Spirit, even before his birth. And he will turn many Israelites to the Lord their God. He will be a man with the spirit and power of Elijah. He will prepare the people for the coming of the Lord. He will turn the hearts of the fathers to their children, and he will cause those who are rebellious to accept the wisdom of the godly."*

*Zechariah said to the angel, "How can I be sure this will happen? I'm an old man now, and my wife is also well along in years."*

*Then the angel said, "I am Gabriel! I stand in the very presence of God. It was he who sent me to bring you this good news! But now, since you didn't believe what I said, you will be silent and unable to speak until the child is born. For my words will certainly be fulfilled at the proper time."*

*Meanwhile, the people were waiting for Zechariah to come out of the sanctuary, wondering why he was taking so long. When he finally did come out, he couldn't speak to them. Then they realized from his gestures and his silence that he must have seen a vision in the sanctuary.*

*When Zechariah's week of service in the Temple was over, he returned home. Soon afterward his wife, Elizabeth, became pregnant and went into seclusion for five months. "How kind the Lord is!" she exclaimed. "He has taken away my disgrace of having no children."*

## LIFE LESSONS

God often works in unexpected ways. Sometimes we don't recognize news or circumstances as the blessings they are until far later. When God sent Gabriel to announce a life-changing development for a far greater future, something that didn't even seem possible, Zechariah couldn't take it in—it was too much. The unlikely path God chose for introducing Jesus to the world came as a shock to Zechariah. The larger plan, though, would alter the course of humankind.

Sometimes our immediate reactions to news or events can make things harder than they need to be. Zechariah refused to accept Gabriel's words, and, as a result, he spent months unable to converse with his wife during her pregnancy. Those months could have been so much easier for both of them if Zechariah had kept his heart open to God's work in his life.

As you go through life's ups and downs, try to take a moment to let your experiences sink in. Keep your heart as open as you can. Instead of resigning yourself to your current situation because it's the one you know, open your heart to new opportunities and potential changes. Imagine the possibilities! It would be a shame if you missed out on a miracle when it came knocking because you were reluctant to open the door.

## WHERE ARE YOU?

*When have you received surprising news?*

_____

_____

_____

_____

_____

*What was your reaction to it?*

_____

_____

_____

_____

_____

*When have you felt overwhelmed by news? How did you work through that experience?*

_____

_____

_____

_____

_____

## A PRAYER

Father, thank You for working in miraculous ways! I pray that I would stay open to opportunities and new circumstances and not just stick to my comfort zone. Please give me the patience for when I don't understand so I can be open to Your blessings and pathway for my life. In Jesus's name, amen.

## DAY 3:
## COURAGE IN ACCEPTANCE

## SCRIPTURE READING

LUKE 1:26–38 (NIV)

*In the sixth month of Elizabeth's pregnancy, God sent the angel Gabriel to Nazareth, a town in Galilee, to a virgin pledged to be married to a man named Joseph, a descendant of David. The virgin's name was Mary. The angel went to her and said, "Greetings, you who are highly favored! The Lord is with you."*

*Mary was greatly troubled at his words and wondered what kind of greeting this might be. But the angel said to her, "Do not be afraid, Mary; you have found favor with God. You will conceive and give birth to a son, and you are to call him Jesus. He will be great and will be called the Son of the Most High. The Lord God will give him the throne of his father David, and he will reign over Jacob's descendants forever; his kingdom will never end."*

*"How will this be," Mary asked the angel, "since I am a virgin?"*

*The angel answered, "The Holy Spirit will come on you, and the power of the Most High will overshadow you. So the holy one to be born will be called the Son of God. Even Elizabeth your relative is going to have a child in her old age, and she who was said to be unable to conceive is in her sixth month. For no word from God will ever fail."*

*"I am the Lord's servant," Mary answered. "May your word to me be fulfilled." Then the angel left her.*

## LIFE LESSONS

Mary discovered that her entire life was about to be shaken up and turned upside down: she was carrying the *Son of God!* Mary probably knew the road ahead wouldn't be easy for her. Pregnancy and child-rearing are difficult journeys to undertake. Yet she replied with graceful acceptance and genuine hope for God's promise. What a response!

Fear of the unknown can be paralyzing. Fear can make it difficult to face even positive changes or additions in our lives. We might respond by rejecting the changes out of hand or by curling up inside ourselves, trying to protect what we already have. We might try to cling to the familiarity of our current life course. Responding to change with fear is understandable, and we can all relate—but it can also limit us.

Ultimately, we don't always get to choose which path to take in life, but we can decide how we're going to respond as we face the unknown. As you keep pressing on through this ninety-day journey with Jesus, look back at Mary's courageous acceptance of her circumstances. The journey ahead might come with some significant changes, but the strength to respond with the same grace Mary did is within you.

## WHERE ARE YOU?

*What has been the most memorable event in your life experience?*

_____

_____

_____

_____

_____

*How old were you? Where were you?*

_____

_____

_____

_____

_____

*What did you do? How did you respond?*

_____

_____

_____

_____

_____

## A PRAYER

Thank You, Lord, for being Jehovah-Shammah, the God who is there. I pray for courage like Mary's, that I wouldn't give in to fear but would instead accept the unexpected with grace and hope. In Your name, amen.

# DAY 4:
## A GREATER JOY

## SCRIPTURE READING

LUKE 1:39–45 (NIV)

*At that time Mary got ready and hurried to a town in the hill country of Judea, where she entered Zechariah's home and greeted Elizabeth. When Elizabeth heard Mary's greeting, the baby leaped in her womb, and Elizabeth was filled with the Holy Spirit. In a loud voice she exclaimed: "Blessed are you among women, and blessed is the child you will bear! But why am I so favored, that the mother of my Lord should come to me? As soon as the sound of your greeting reached my ears, the baby in my womb leaped for joy. Blessed is she who has believed that the Lord would fulfill his promises to her!"*

## LIFE LESSONS

Carrying joy within yourself is a wonderful feeling, but sharing joy feels even better. There's nothing like sharing good news with a friend or family member. Today's passage is all about joy: both the joy that Mary and Elizabeth received as they shared good news and the joy we take in knowing that the baby Mary carried would become our Savior who delights to share in our joy.

Mary and Elizabeth were, understandably, incredibly excited about Jesus's presence in their lives. The scene of Mary sharing her news with Elizabeth is one of joyful anticipation. These two women would have the privilege of knowing Jesus intimately—and we share that same privilege today. Christ delights in our achievements, our well-being, our happiness, and our good days. He's always excited for our wins—never jealous, never downplaying our efforts. We can always share those moments with Him.

Shared joy can become something so much greater and connect us in ways we didn't know were possible, so don't hold back; share away!

## WHERE ARE YOU?

*Why do you think Mary traveled to Elizabeth's home?*

_____

_____

_____

_____

_____

*Think back to a big accomplishment or event in your life. With whom did you share the news? How did they respond?*

_____

_____

_____

_____

_____

*How does it feel to know that Jesus delights in your achievements?*

_____

_____

_____

_____

_____

## A PRAYER

Jesus, thank You for always being there, listening, and celebrating my achievements alongside me. Remind me to share my joy with You when good things happen. I also pray for a solid community of friends who will lift me up through the good and the bad. In Your name, amen.

# DAY 5:
## MORE CELEBRATION, MORE APPRECIATION

## SCRIPTURE READING

LUKE 1:46–56 (NIV)

*And Mary said:*

> *"My soul glorifies the Lord*
>   *and my spirit rejoices in God my Savior,*
>
> *for he has been mindful*
>   *of the humble state of his servant.*
>
> *From now on all generations will call me blessed,*
>   *for the Mighty One has done great things for me—*
>   *holy is his name.*
>
> *His mercy extends to those who fear him,*
>   *from generation to generation.*
>
> *He has performed mighty deeds with his arm;*
>   *he has scattered those who are proud in their inmost thoughts.*
>
> *He has brought down rulers from their thrones*
>   *but has lifted up the humble.*
>
> *He has filled the hungry with good things*
>   *but has sent the rich away empty.*
>
> *He has helped his servant Israel,*
>   *remembering to be merciful*
> *to Abraham and his descendants forever,*
>   *just as he promised our ancestors."*

*Mary stayed with Elizabeth for about three months and then returned home.*

## LIFE LESSONS

We should take time to regularly celebrate the good things in our lives. Celebrating helps us appreciate what we have, and it makes our time here on earth far more enjoyable. Deliberately recognizing and reflecting on what's going well refocuses us and gives us the strength to keep going.

The song of praise that Mary sings here, while she is pregnant with Jesus, and while her cousin Elizabeth is pregnant with John the Baptist, is known as the Magnificat, Latin for "my soul magnifies the Lord"—a nod to the song's powerful opening line. It's Mary's response to what God has done for her and will do in her future. We can learn a lot from Mary's posture of worship as she throws herself into celebrating the life and good things God has bestowed upon her.

The Magnificat is Mary's celebration of Christ coming into the world. We can join Mary in her celebrating because Jesus is still here in the world with us.

## WHERE ARE YOU?

*What lines from Mary's Magnificat stand out to you?*

_____

_____

_____

_____

_____

*What's the best news you've ever received? How did you learn about it?*
*Who told you?*

_____

_____

_____

_____

_____

*How can celebrating achievements encourage us in difficult times?*

_____

_____

_____

_____

_____

## A PRAYER

Lord Jesus, thank You for Mary and her faith in You, and for her significant example of praise and joy. Remind me to celebrate life along the way and to thank You along the way as well. In Your name, amen.

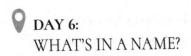

# DAY 6:
## WHAT'S IN A NAME?

## SCRIPTURE READING

LUKE 1:57–66 (NIV)

*When it was time for Elizabeth to have her baby, she gave birth to a son. Her neighbors and relatives heard that the Lord had shown her great mercy, and they shared her joy.*

*On the eighth day they came to circumcise the child, and they were going to name him after his father Zechariah, but his mother spoke up and said, "No! He is to be called John."*

*They said to her, "There is no one among your relatives who has that name."*

*Then they made signs to his father, to find out what he would like to name the child. He asked for a writing tablet, and to everyone's astonishment he wrote, "His name is John." Immediately his mouth was opened and his tongue set free, and he began to speak, praising God. All the neighbors were filled with awe, and throughout the hill country of Judea people were talking about all these things. Everyone who heard this wondered about it, asking, "What then is this child going to be?" For the Lord's hand was with him.*

## LIFE LESSONS

Names are powerful. They identify us, they influence how people perceive us, they trace our bloodlines, and they're what we're remembered by when we're long gone. Our names trail us everywhere we go, and sometimes they even go before us our entire life here and beyond.

In this story, it's not just what's in a name; it's also what's in a promise. God not only calls us by name, but His promises are for us as well. John the Baptist was born to point people to Jesus—the Name above all names—and God, knowing he would do just that, knew exactly what He wanted John's name to be. John's name would go before him, a beacon pointing to the coming of Jesus.

When Zechariah broke tradition and wrote the name "John," God kept His promise and brought back Zechariah's voice. God moved in response to Zechariah and Elizabeth's faithfulness and trust. They believed in the promise of God and that everyone down the road would remember their son's name, even if it wasn't a family name. John's name is a powerful reminder that God always makes good on His promises.

## WHERE ARE YOU?

*Why was Zechariah's insistence on naming his child John significant?*

_____

_____

_____

_____

*What does your name mean? Do you know why your parents chose it for you?*

_____

_____

_____

_____

*In what ways is John's name a reminder that God keeps His promises?*

_____

_____

_____

_____

_____

## A PRAYER

Father God, thank You for calling me by name, and thank You for being a promise-making, promise-keeping God. You are the reason for my hope and my future because You always make good on Your promises. Amen.

# DAY 7:
## WORTH THE WAIT

## SCRIPTURE READING

LUKE 1:67–80 (NLT)

Then his father, Zechariah, was filled with the Holy Spirit and gave this prophecy:

"Praise the Lord, the God of Israel,
  because he has visited and redeemed his people.

He has sent us a mighty Savior
  from the royal line of his servant David,
just as he promised
  through his holy prophets long ago.
Now we will be saved from our enemies
  and from all who hate us.
He has been merciful to our ancestors
  by remembering his sacred covenant—
the covenant he swore with an oath
  to our ancestor Abraham.
We have been rescued from our enemies
  so we can serve God without fear,
in holiness and righteousness
  for as long as we live.

"And you, my little son,
  will be called the prophet of the Most High,
  because you will prepare the way for the Lord.
You will tell his people how to find salvation
  through forgiveness of their sins.
Because of God's tender mercy,
  the morning light from heaven is about to break upon us,
to give light to those who sit in darkness and in the shadow of death,
  and to guide us to the path of peace."

John grew up and became strong in spirit. And he lived in the wilderness until he began his public ministry to Israel.

## LIFE LESSONS

Waiting. Most of us aren't huge fans of it. Holding on for a known amount of time can be hard enough. Waiting an unknown amount of time—or, worse, experiencing a delay—can be unbearable. The truth is, patience is a hard-earned trait, especially when we know something great is on its way. Sometimes the journey accompanying an expectation or hope can feel impossible. That moment we're done waiting, though? That second when what we were waiting for comes to fruition? There is nothing quite like it.

Elizabeth and Zechariah both had to wait for their son to be born, but their experiences of that waiting period differed. Elizabeth spent those months in hopeful anticipation, watching her body transform as new life grew inside her. Zechariah, on the other hand, spent those months in silence. Can you imagine the joy they both felt upon seeing God's promise fulfilled? For Zechariah, John's birth ushered in the return of his voice along with the absolute assurance that his son would pave the way for the Lord and Savior. When Zechariah first laid eyes on John, he could be certain that the Lord and Savior was *coming* to earth.

Jesus is our hope. He is the promise sent down from heaven to meet us where we are. At times it can be difficult to wait on God to act in our lives, but we must hold on to hope, just as Zechariah did. The wait will be worth it.

## WHERE ARE YOU?

*What lines from Zechariah's prophecy stand out to you?*

_____

_____

_____

_____

_____

*What is something for which you waited a long time? How did you respond when it arrived?*

_____

_____

_____

_____

_____

*What sustains you when you're in a period of waiting?*

_____

_____

_____

_____

_____

## A PRAYER

Jesus, thank You for coming to us. Thank You for bringing genuine hope into the world. I pray for patience in my everyday life and a renewed sense of hope each morning so that I can live the way You intended for Your children to live. In Your name, amen.

# DAY 8:
## WOVEN GRACE

## SCRIPTURE READING

MATTHEW 1:1–6 (MSG)

*The family tree of Jesus Christ, David's son, Abraham's son:*

*Abraham had Isaac,*

*Isaac had Jacob,*

*Jacob had Judah and his brothers,*

*Judah had Perez and Zerah (the mother was Tamar),*

*Perez had Hezron,*

*Hezron had Aram,*

*Aram had Amminadab,*

*Amminadab had Nahshon,*

*Nahshon had Salmon,*

*Salmon had Boaz (his mother was Rahab),*

*Boaz had Obed (Ruth was the mother),*

*Obed had Jesse,*

*Jesse had David, and David became king.*

*David had Solomon (Uriah's wife was the mother).*

SEE ALSO: MATTHEW 1:7–17; LUKE 3:23–38

## LIFE LESSONS

Family. For better or for worse, we all come from families. We are each descended from ancestors and part of an extensive family history and family tree. Matthew 1 shows us the genealogy of Jesus Christ, and, boy, does He have an extensive family history! It is full of ups and downs and interesting characters.

We can learn a lot from a family tree, and Jesus's tree is no exception. It shows that Christ is a descendant of David and Abraham, and as such He fulfills the prophecies of the Old Testament. Matthew emphasizes Jesus's lineage, using the phrase "Son of David" ten times to describe Jesus. The apostle Paul's description of Abraham as the "Father of our faith" in Romans 4:1 similarly reminds us of Jesus's heritage among God's chosen people.

Like most families, Jesus's family history is marked by both scandal and incredible tales of transformation. Grace is woven throughout the genealogy of Jesus: God used every single person in this family tree, over the course of time, to change the world. Regardless of who they were and what mistakes they made, God allowed something incredible to come out of them.

God can use each one of us in incredible ways too. He looks beyond all our brokenness and all the areas in which the world says we are insufficient, and He *knows* our potential, even when no one else seems to. As we walk each day with Jesus, He can show us how His grace truly is sufficient. When you put your faith in God, He can transform anything.

## WHERE ARE YOU?

*What names do you recognize from Jesus's family tree? Did any of the names surprise you?*

_____

_____

_____

_____

_____

*How do you see your family history influencing you?*

_____

_____

_____

_____

_____

*How does it feel to know that people who made mistakes are part of Jesus's lineage?*

_____

_____

_____

_____

_____

## A PRAYER

Dear God, thank You for showing us Your transformative power and grace through Christ's genealogy. We can be broken, and You can use us all the same. Thank You for Your never-ending belief in us and our capabilities. In Jesus's name, amen.

**DAY 9:**
# AN EXTRAORDINARY "ORDINARY" MIRACLE

## SCRIPTURE READING

LUKE 2:1–7 (MSG)

*About that time Caesar Augustus ordered a census to be taken throughout the Empire. This was the first census when Quirinius was governor of Syria. Everyone had to travel to his own ancestral hometown to be accounted for. So Joseph went from the Galilean town of Nazareth up to Bethlehem in Judah, David's town, for the census. As a descendant of David, he had to go there. He went with Mary, his fiancée, who was pregnant.*

*While they were there, the time came for her to give birth. She gave birth to a son, her firstborn. She wrapped him in a blanket and laid him in a manger, because there was no room in the hostel.*

SEE ALSO: MATTHEW 1:18–25

## LIFE LESSONS

There is nothing unique about being born, but there is absolutely something miraculous about it. No, Jesus's birth wasn't the only miracle birth. Pregnancy and childbirth are miracles all on their own, making our existence on this earth worth celebrating.

Although the birth of Christ *is* unique, unlike any other, and the yearly commemoration of His birth has become a large celebration spanning countries and cultures, God sent Jesus to be born in a plain, ordinary way. His birth was an extraordinary "ordinary" miracle. The Messiah, God's only Son, was born to simple people—a carpenter and his fiancée—in a manner no one expected for the future Savior of the world. Indeed, Mary and Joseph probably had a rough time of it: they were alone, without a place to stay, and their unmarried status would have turned the birth into a scandal. And yet, Jesus's birth changed the lives of everyone who would ever pass through this world.

God specifically prepared Jesus's story and life to resemble the *entire* measure of the human experience, beginning with His human birth. God has His own purposes and plans for us as well, no matter how ordinary our own beginnings may seem.

## WHERE ARE YOU?

*Do you know your own birth story? If so, relate what happened.*

_____

_____

_____

_____

_____

*How do you and your family celebrate Christmas?*

_____

_____

_____

_____

_____

*What are some of your memories of the Christmas holiday season, good or bad?*

_____

_____

_____

_____

_____

## A PRAYER

Father God, thank You for sending Jesus to a young couple who trusted in Your plan. It's incredible how You use ordinary situations and ordinary people for extraordinary outcomes. I'm so grateful You sent Your Son here to live among us. In Jesus's name, amen.

# DAY 10:
## HERE FOR EVERYONE

## SCRIPTURE READING

LUKE 2:8–20 (NIV)

*And there were shepherds living out in the fields nearby, keeping watch over their flocks at night. An angel of the Lord appeared to them, and the glory of the Lord shone around them, and they were terrified. But the angel said to them, "Do not be afraid. I bring you good news that will cause great joy for all the people. Today in the town of David a Savior has been born to you; he is the Messiah, the Lord. This will be a sign to you: You will find a baby wrapped in cloths and lying in a manger."*

*Suddenly a great company of the heavenly host appeared with the angel, praising God and saying, "Glory to God in the highest heaven, and on earth peace to those on whom his favor rests." When the angels had left them and gone into heaven, the shepherds said to one another, "Let's go to Bethlehem and see this thing that has happened, which the Lord has told us about."*

*So they hurried off and found Mary and Joseph, and the baby, who was lying in the manger. When they had seen him, they spread the word concerning what had been told them about this child, and all who heard it were amazed at what the shepherds said to them. But Mary treasured up all these things and pondered them in her heart. The shepherds returned, glorifying and praising God for all the things they had heard and seen, which were just as they had been told.*

## LIFE LESSONS

Two distinct groups of people visited Jesus when He was either a baby or a young toddler: shepherds and *"scholars from the East"* (Matthew 2:7 MSG). God chose two extremes of society to welcome His Son into the world, signaling from the very beginning that Jesus had been sent to redeem *all* people.

Both visiting groups faced hardships to meet the new Savior. The shepherds, on the lower rungs of society, were privileged to be invited by angels, a heavenly party announcing the long-awaited coming of the Messiah. Once invited, though, the shepherds knew they would have to leave behind their flocks and trust that the journey would be worth it. The Magi from the East dealt with distance, rough terrain, and having to outwit a suspicious ruler before arriving, all while following a star they just *knew* was important.

God brought His Son down to earth for everybody, the full spectrum of society, regardless of where we fall or if we bump up or down along the way. Everyone will have their own journey, and each one of us will encounter hardships, but Christ will be waiting to meet us on our own time and in our own way, accepting us just as we are.

## WHERE ARE YOU?

*What significance lies in the two groups of people who visited Jesus as a baby or a young boy?*

_____

_____

_____

_____

_____

*What challenges have you faced to meet and follow the Savior?*

_____

_____

_____

_____

_____

*How does the knowledge that Jesus came for everyone affect how you see others?*

_____

_____

_____

_____

_____

## A PRAYER

Father God, thank You for calling people from all places and circumstances to follow You. I praise You because You came for every person, as we are all in need of Your strength, love, and mercy. Help me to worship You because You deserve our worship every day, through every step of the journey. In Your name, amen.

# DAY 11:
## A REVELATION IN A NAME

## SCRIPTURE READING

LUKE 2:21 (NIV)

*On the eighth day, when it was time to circumcise the child, he was named Jesus, the name the angel had given him before he was conceived.*

## LIFE LESSONS

In our society, people often select a name for their baby weeks, if not months, before they are born. The parents may share the name on social media and in a formal announcement in anticipation of the child's arrival, and they may include artwork with the baby's name with their decorations for the nursery. People select baby names for a variety of reasons: sometimes parents choose a name because they like the sound of it, other times they pick a name with familial history, and sometimes they're motivated by a name's meaning or significance. Whether the name recalls a character from a favorite book or movie, brings to mind a figure in history, or holds significance in its translation or root meaning, there is generally a purpose behind each name. Sometimes a name can even reveal the parents' expectations for the newborn child.

In biblical times, names were extremely important and were always chosen for very specific reasons. A naming ceremony took place for a child eight days after they were born, and the entire village would turn out for the proclamation. On two occasions before the birth of Jesus, an angel told Joseph and Mary what they were to name their child. And, much like He did for John, God used the name of Jesus for something special.

God revealed His grand plan when He instructed that His Son be named Jesus, meaning "God saves." Both Jesus's future and ours were written into His very name. It was a significant designation declaring Jesus's path as well as our own paths under God's grace.

## WHERE ARE YOU?

*If you are a parent, why did you choose the name(s) you selected for your child(ren)?*

_____
_____
_____
_____
_____

*Why do you think the name of Jesus is important?*

_____
_____
_____
_____
_____

*What does Jesus's name mean to you?*

_____
_____
_____
_____
_____

## A PRAYER

Jesus, "God saves," thank You for the forgiveness, hope, and healing found in Your name. I praise You for living up to Your name and bringing us all into Your light. In Your name I pray, amen.

# DAY 12:
## THE LAST LAMB

## SCRIPTURE READING

LUKE 2:22–24 (MSG)

*Then when the days stipulated by Moses for purification were complete, they took him up to Jerusalem to offer him to God as commanded in God's Law: "Every male who opens the womb shall be a holy offering to God," and also to sacrifice the "pair of doves or two young pigeons" prescribed in God's Law.*

## LIFE LESSONS

Before Christ's arrival, being part of God's people meant following extensive rules for purification and atonement of sin. At that time, laws and sacrifices were the people's only means for redeeming themselves and drawing closer to God. In the gospel of Luke, we see Joseph and Mary, devout Jews, carrying out the sacrifices God had commanded be made following the birth of a child.

According to Leviticus 12:2–8, a mother was unclean for the first seven days after giving birth to a son. On the eighth day, the son would be circumcised. The mother would have to wait another thirty-three days to be considered fully purified. After a total of forty days since giving birth, the mother could finally go to the temple for the purification ceremony. She was required to bring a lamb for a burnt offering and a young pigeon or turtledove as a sin offering. If she couldn't afford a sacrificial lamb, she could substitute another pigeon or turtledove in its place. This offered even the most marginalized families the privilege of purification.

Too poor to do otherwise, Mary offered the two birds to satisfy both requirements. She had no literal lamb to offer. Even so, she *did* bring a lamb. She brought the "Lamb of God," who would end up fulfilling all of these laws, bringing them under a different light, and negating the need for blood sacrifices. In essence, she brought the last lamb we would ever need.

## WHERE ARE YOU?

*Why did Jesus's parents take Him to Jerusalem when He was an infant?*

_____

_____

_____

_____

_____

*What was the significance of Mary bringing two turtledoves instead of a lamb as her sacrificial offering?*

_____

_____

_____

_____

_____

*Because of Jesus, what is our means of redemption and atonement for sin?*

_____

_____

_____

_____

_____

## A PRAYER

Jesus, thank You for being the offering, the final lamb to atone for our sins forever. Thank You for making it possible for us to be closer to God through Your sacrifice. Help me to show my gratefulness even when I don't have the words. In Your name, amen.

# DAY 13:
## KEEP HOLDING ON

## SCRIPTURE READING

LUKE 2:25–35 (MSG)

*In Jerusalem at the time, there was a man, Simeon by name, a good man, a man who lived in the prayerful expectancy of help for Israel. And the Holy Spirit was on him. The Holy Spirit had shown him that he would see the Messiah of God before he died. Led by the Spirit, he entered the Temple. As the parents of the child Jesus brought him in to carry out the rituals of the Law, Simeon took him into his arms and blessed God:*

> *God, you can now release your servant;*
> *release me in peace as you promised.*
> *With my own eyes I've seen your salvation;*
> *it's now out in the open for everyone to see:*
> *A God-revealing light to the non-Jewish nations,*
> *and of glory for your people Israel.*

*Jesus's father and mother were speechless with surprise at these words. Simeon went on to bless them, and said to Mary his mother,*

> *This child marks both the failure and*
> *the recovery of many in Israel,*
> *A figure misunderstood and contradicted—*
> *the pain of a sword-thrust through you—*
> *But the rejection will force honesty,*
> *as God reveals who they really are.*

## LIFE LESSONS

Time spent waiting for a promise to be fulfilled can seem to drag on and on. It's a quest all on its own, with ups and downs, hesitations, and misgivings. So much can happen in your life while you wait. There's a distinct sensation of uncertainty that comes with it: *Is it ever going to happen? Should I keep waiting? Am I wasting my time?* When you're not sure, you really have to throw yourself in and keep believing no matter what.

Simeon's conviction, his belief in God's promise and the coming of the Messiah, stayed with him all the way to old age. He continued to hold on. Can you imagine the relief and the joy he felt at finally seeing that promise come to fruition? What bliss must have filled him to know that all his waiting had been worthwhile. What peace must have flooded him, realizing the wait was over.

Holding on to Jesus's promises may come with uncertainty and some creeping doubt, but forge ahead. It may take a while, it may even feel like it's taking too long, but you have nothing to lose and everything to gain by holding fast.

## WHERE ARE YOU?

*What is something you've waited a long time for?*

_____
_____
_____
_____

*In your view, what was Simeon waiting for?*

_____
_____
_____
_____
_____

*What are some things Simeon said Jesus was destined to cause?*

_____
_____
_____
_____

## A PRAYER

Lord Jesus, give me the strength to wait because I know You always keep Your promises. I know there will be uncertainty along the way, but I want to be open to Your lead. Help me to overcome my doubts when they show up, and fill me with Your positive assurance instead. In Your name, amen.

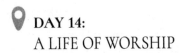

# DAY 14:
# A LIFE OF WORSHIP

## SCRIPTURE READING

LUKE 2:36–39 (NLT)

*Anna, a prophet, was also there in the Temple. She was the daughter of Phanuel from the tribe of Asher, and she was very old. Her husband died when they had been married only seven years. Then she lived as a widow to the age of eighty-four. She never left the Temple but stayed there day and night, worshiping God with fasting and prayer. She came along just as Simeon was talking with Mary and Joseph, and she began praising God. She talked about the child to everyone who had been waiting expectantly for God to rescue Jerusalem.*

*When Jesus's parents had fulfilled all the requirements of the law of the Lord, they returned home to Nazareth in Galilee.*

## LIFE LESSONS

The prophetess Anna lived as a widow for eighty-four years, during which time she never left the temple. God was her life. Nothing else mattered to her except spending time in His presence in that place of worship. Her unwavering commitment to God and to worshipping Him led her to be at the right place at the right time. While she was doing what she always did, resting in the presence of God, she got to experience one of the most poignant moments in history.

God rewards those who diligently seek Him and spend time in His presence.

Worship can mean a lot of different things. It can take the form of singing, prayer, enjoying the beauty of nature and praising God for it, speaking about God with others, reading about Jesus, or even sitting silently and meditating. There are so many possibilities, and not everyone feels led in the same direction. What makes your soul feel happy and close to God may not do it for someone else. Ultimately, worship is simply about focusing on God and being in His presence. The more we do it, the wider our hearts open, and the more we align ourselves with God's plans for us.

## WHERE ARE YOU?

*In your view, what is "worship"?*

_____
_____
_____
_____
_____

*How did Anna worship God?*

_____
_____
_____
_____
_____

*Whom did Anna tell about Jesus?*

_____
_____
_____
_____
_____

## A PRAYER

Jesus, thank You for rewarding faith and revealing Yourself to Your servants. Show me more ways to connect with You every day. Don't let me fall into the trap of limiting or restricting the ways in which I worship You. Help me to find forms of worship that allow me to seek You and praise You with all my heart. In Your name, amen.

# DAY 15:
## START WALKING

## SCRIPTURE READING

.....................................................................................................

### MATTHEW 2:1–12 (MSG)

*After Jesus was born in Bethlehem village, Judah territory—this was during Herod's kingship—a band of scholars arrived in Jerusalem from the East. They asked around, "Where can we find and pay homage to the newborn King of the Jews? We observed a star in the eastern sky that signaled his birth. We're on pilgrimage to worship him."*

*When word of their inquiry got to Herod, he was terrified—and not Herod alone, but most of Jerusalem as well. Herod lost no time. He gathered all the high priests and religion scholars in the city together and asked, "Where is the Messiah supposed to be born?"*

*They told him, "Bethlehem, Judah territory. The prophet Micah wrote it plainly:*

> *It's you, Bethlehem, in Judah's land,*
> > *no longer bringing up the rear.*
> *From you will come the leader*
> > *who will shepherd-rule my people, my Israel."*

*Herod then arranged a secret meeting with the scholars from the East. Pretending to be as devout as they were, he got them to tell him exactly when the birth-announcement star appeared. Then he told them the prophecy about Bethlehem, and said, "Go find this child. Leave no stone unturned. As soon as you find him, send word and I'll join you at once in your worship."*

*Instructed by the king, they set off. Then the star appeared again, the same star they had seen in the eastern skies. It led them on until it hovered over the place of the child. They could hardly contain themselves: They were in the right place! They had arrived at the right time!*

*They entered the house and saw the child in the arms of Mary, his mother. Overcome, they kneeled and worshiped him. Then they opened their luggage and presented gifts: gold, frankincense, myrrh.*

*In a dream, they were warned not to report back to Herod. So they worked out another route, left the territory without being seen, and returned to their own country.*

## LIFE LESSONS

Being led seems easy—but it isn't always. We may stop paying attention and end up in the wrong place or become sidetracked by something that takes us off our destined path. Sometimes where we end up seems all wrong, and we start having doubts. Someone else may attempt to deter us entirely. Trusting our guide and allowing ourselves to be led is often the hardest part.

Matthew tells us that when several wise, powerful men from the kingdom of Persia saw a star rise, they got on their feet, packed belongings for a long journey, and headed out, not knowing where they would end up. God called to them, and they responded. They stopped at King Herod's palace, which wasn't the right place at all, and discovered that not everyone was happy about the newborn King of the Jews. God continued to guide the wise men, and they continued to follow as He directed them away from Herod and toward the true King.

The wise men had the star to guide them, but they still had to trust in the star, have faith that they would end up in the right spot, and believe this exhausting journey would be worth the effort. Spoiler: it was. Their journey ended in utter joy as they met the newborn King.

In Jesus, we find a guide who is trustworthy. Jesus is interested in all of us, no matter our status in society or the distance we may travel to find and follow Him. And His path leads us to where we are meant to be. We still have to take that first step, though, and start walking.

## WHERE ARE YOU?

*What did the wise men ask when they arrived in Jerusalem?*

*What happened when the wise men found Jesus?*

_____

_____

_____

_____

_____

*How did the wise men ultimately respond to Herod's request? Why?*

_____

_____

_____

_____

_____

## A PRAYER

Jesus, thank You for Your love. I pray that the same joy that was shown at Your birth might fill every encounter I have with You. I pray for strength for the journey ahead. Use me to change the world today and every day. In Your name, amen.

## DAY 16:
## GET UP AND DO IT

## SCRIPTURE READING

MATTHEW 2:13–18 (MSG)

*After the scholars were gone, God's angel showed up again in Joseph's dream and commanded, "Get up. Take the child and his mother and flee to Egypt. Stay until further notice. Herod is on the hunt for this child, and wants to kill him."*

*Joseph obeyed. He got up, took the child and his mother under cover of darkness. They were out of town and well on their way by daylight. They lived in Egypt until Herod's death. This Egyptian exile fulfilled what Hosea had preached: "I called my son out of Egypt."*

*Herod, when he realized that the scholars had tricked him, flew into a rage. He commanded the murder of every little boy two years old and under who lived in Bethlehem and its surrounding hills. (He determined that age from information he'd gotten from the scholars.) That's when Jeremiah's revelation was fulfilled:*

> *A sound was heard in Ramah,*
>> *weeping and much lament.*
> *Rachel weeping for her children,*
>> *Rachel refusing all solace,*
> *Her children gone,*
>> *dead and buried.*

## LIFE LESSONS

Would you be ready to leave your current life and start a new journey at a moment's notice? What if doing so was necessary in order to protect the people you love? You could call Joseph's faith walk a "get up and do it" journey.

Joseph didn't have the luxury of whining or overthinking things. When God told him to do something, he got up and did it. Joseph didn't understand everything about his circumstances. He didn't know where each step would lead or what would come after, and he didn't know how his family's presence might affect the community around them. But he trusted God anyway and did what was asked of him to keep his family safe.

Joseph's obedience to God's instructions saved his child from a cruel fate no one deserved. It also saved himself and his wife, Mary, from experiencing the horrible grief and misfortune that fell on every other parent of a young boy in Bethlehem.

We can't control how others act. We can only control our own actions. God doesn't determine anyone's actions—we make our own decisions. And we can never know what will happen next or how our decisions will affect others. What we *can* do is put our hope in Christ and His plans for us and keep following Him.

## WHERE ARE YOU?

*This is a tough passage for many people. When have you faced grief?*

*What motivated Herod's violent decree?*

*How did Herod's terrible intentions fulfill prophecy?*

## A PRAYER

Jesus, thank You for the example of amazing faith You have given us in Joseph. Help me to trust Your promises and plan even when I don't understand. Increase my faith, Lord. In Your name, amen.

# DAY 17:
## PLANS AND PREPARATIONS

## SCRIPTURE READINGS

MATTHEW 2:19–23 (MSG)

*Later, when Herod died, God's angel appeared in a dream to Joseph in Egypt: "Up, take the child and his mother and return to Israel. All those out to murder the child are dead."*

*Joseph obeyed. He got up, took the child and his mother, and reentered Israel. When he heard, though, that Archelaus had succeeded his father, Herod, as king in Judea, he was afraid to go there. But then Joseph was directed in a dream to go to the hills of Galilee. On arrival, he settled in the village of Nazareth. This move was a fulfillment of the prophetic words, "He shall be called a Nazarene."*

LUKE 2:40 (MSG)

*There the child grew strong in body and wise in spirit. And the grace of God was on him.*

## LIFE LESSONS

Life can often feel like it's all over the place. We're here, we're there, we've lost our job, we're starting a new one in a different field—life just keeps sweeping us along in a current of circumstances outside of our control. Through all the madness, and sometimes through the pain, it can be comforting to know that Someone has a plan, even if we don't. There are no coincidences with God. He knows where we're headed and how we'll get there, even if the ensuing events don't make sense to us at the time (or possibly ever).

God's planning can be readily seen in His preparations for sending Jesus. He knew that convincing the world that Jesus really is His Son would be essential, so He ensured that Scripture would pave the way: the Old Testament contains more than three hundred prophecies about Jesus. That's a heavy preplanning strategy! The statistical probability of one man fulfilling all three hundred prophecies perfectly is astronomical. One study stated that there would be a one in a quadrillion chance that one person could fulfill just *eight* of those prophecies. Jesus Christ fulfilled *all* three hundred exactly as Scripture had predicted.

God had a plan for the birth and life of Jesus. He has a plan for you too.

## WHERE ARE YOU?

*What is something in your life that beats great odds?*

_____
_____
_____
_____
_____

*Why is it important that Jesus is called "Jesus of Nazareth"?*

_____
_____
_____
_____
_____

*Have you ever had a sense that God has a plan for your life?*

_____
_____
_____
_____
_____

## A PRAYER

Father God, thank You for always having a plan. Help me to trust in that plan, even when life feels hard or directionless. Thank You for inspiring the authors of the Old Testament to write down what would take place years before it occurred. The proof of who You are is undeniable. In Jesus's name, amen.

# DAY 18:
## STOP AND THINK

## SCRIPTURE READING

LUKE 2:41–50 (NLT)

*Every year Jesus's parents went to Jerusalem for the Passover festival. When Jesus was twelve years old, they attended the festival as usual. After the celebration was over, they started home to Nazareth, but Jesus stayed behind in Jerusalem. His parents didn't miss him at first, because they assumed he was among the other travelers. But when he didn't show up that evening, they started looking for him among their relatives and friends.*

*When they couldn't find him, they went back to Jerusalem to search for him there. Three days later they finally discovered him in the Temple, sitting among the religious teachers, listening to them and asking questions. All who heard him were amazed at his understanding and his answers.*

*His parents didn't know what to think. "Son," his mother said to him, "why have you done this to us? Your father and I have been frantic, searching for you everywhere."*

*"But why did you need to search?" he asked. "Didn't you know that I must be in my Father's house?" But they didn't understand what he meant.*

## LIFE LESSONS

Any parent whose child has gone missing in a store or at a theme park knows the panic and fear Jesus's parents must have experienced on their way home from Jerusalem. Not only was their child missing, but that child was Jesus. They had lost the *Son of God!* Talk about heavy pressure on first-time parents.

When Mary and Joseph eventually found Jesus in the temple talking with the religious teachers, they reacted as most parents would. They'd been genuinely afraid, searching frantically for three days. So, while they were relieved, they were also upset.

This is the only story we have about Jesus from the period between His birth and the beginning of His ministry at the approximate age of thirty, and it demonstrates His early understanding of His purpose. He essentially said, "Why wouldn't I be here?" In their panic, Mary and Joseph seemed to have forgotten who their Son actually was.

We can't blame Mary for her frantic spirit in the face of fear. Many times when we're upset or scared, our hearts and our heads just don't match up. We react instead of stopping to think; we respond in fear and sometimes end up worse off. We get upset and look everywhere but at Jesus, who is right there before us, waiting to offer us His help and peace. Mary's story reminds us to stop, take a breath, think, and look to Jesus and who He is to guide us.

## WHERE ARE YOU?

*Recall a time you lost something important. What happened? How did you feel?*

_____

_____

_____

_____

_____

*Why would Jesus go to the temple to talk to the teachers?*

_____

_____

_____

_____

*Put yourself in Mary's shoes—how would you react to Jesus's response?*

_____

_____

_____

_____

_____

## A PRAYER

Jesus, forgive me for losing sight of You so many times in my journey of life. Help me to always look to You first and seek You with all my heart. Your Word says that when I do, I will find You. In Your name, amen.

# DAY 19:
## MAKING RIGHT CHOICES

## SCRIPTURE READING

LUKE 2:51–52 (NLT)

*Then he returned to Nazareth with them and was obedient to them. And his mother stored all these things in her heart.*

*Jesus grew in wisdom and in stature and in favor with God and all the people.*

## LIFE LESSONS

We make more decisions every single day than we can even count. Each decision, every small step we take, adds up—whether it's leading us in a potentially new direction or keeping us on the same road we've been on all along. Minor actions influence our life in big ways.

Jesus says that if we want to lead our best life, we must honor our heavenly Father and obey His commands. This is a tall order, and one that often overwhelms us. Yet God's commandments are meant to protect us, not limit us. They're intended to help us build a better future for ourselves and those around us. They prevent us from hurting ourselves and other people, whether physically or emotionally.

As we walk through life with Jesus, we will find that He offers us the strength and counsel to make the right choices—choices that lead to a more fulfilled life that's built on solid relationships and characterized by hope and love.

## WHERE ARE YOU?

*What is a choice that you have made that you feel has had a great impact on your life?*

_____

_____

_____

_____

_____

*What does the word "favor" mean in the verse that describes Jesus "growing in favor" with God and other people?*

_____

_____

_____

_____

_____

*Like Mary, what experiences are you storing up in your heart?*

_____

_____

_____

_____

_____

## A PRAYER

Lord, thank You for guiding me each day with Your protection and love. Help me with the hard decisions and when I'm not sure what to do next. I pray for Your wisdom to live the best life I possibly can. In Jesus's name, amen.

# DAY 20:
## A LONGING FOR RELATIONSHIPS

## SCRIPTURE READING

### JOHN 1:1–5, 10–14, 16–18 (NIV)

*In the beginning was the Word, and the Word was with God, and the Word was God. He was with God in the beginning. Through him all things were made; without him nothing was made that has been made. In him was life, and that life was the light of all mankind. The light shines in the darkness, and the darkness has not overcome it....*

*...He was in the world, and though the world was made through him, the world did not recognize him. He came to that which was his own, but his own did not receive him. Yet to all who did receive him, to those who believed in his name, he gave the right to become children of God—children born not of natural descent, nor of human decision or a husband's will, but born of God.*

*The Word became flesh and made his dwelling among us. We have seen his glory, the glory of the one and only Son, who came from the Father, full of grace and truth....*

*...Out of his fullness we have all received grace in place of grace already given. For the law was given through Moses; grace and truth came through Jesus Christ. No one has ever seen God, but the one and only Son, who is himself God and is in closest relationship with the Father, has made him known.*

## LIFE LESSONS

Whereas Matthew opens his gospel by detailing Jesus's earthly family tree, John begins his book with theology. He establishes that Jesus has always "been" because He is one with God as part of the triune relationship of the Father, Son, and Holy Spirit.

Because we are human, our minds can't fully understand what John is describing. It can be difficult to process how Jesus could have always "been" and how three can be one. But this complex relationship is critical to our understanding of God's love and His sending Jesus to earth.

What it all comes down to is that God desires relationship. The people He created, all made in His image, were *designed* for relationship with Him. This longing to have a relationship with us is exactly why God sent His Son to live here on earth. That is how much He wants to connect with us. That is how much He wants us to know Him.

## WHERE ARE YOU?

*How would you describe your relationship with the person closest to you?*

_____
_____
_____
_____
_____

*What does this text tell us about who God is?*

_____
_____
_____
_____
_____

*What is the connection between God and Jesus in this passage?*

_____
_____
_____
_____
_____

## A PRAYER

I praise You, Jesus, for being the God before creation, the God behind communion, and the God beyond all comprehension. May I always live in awe of You. In Jesus's name, amen.

# DAY 21:
## A LIFE THAT SHINES

## SCRIPTURE READING

JOHN 1:6–9 (NIV)

*There was a man sent from God whose name was John. He came as a witness to testify concerning that light, so that through him all might believe. He himself was not the light; he came only as a witness to the light.*

*The true light that gives light to everyone was coming into the world.*

## LIFE LESSONS

Have you ever sat in a dark room with just a single candle lit? It's incredible how radiant that one small flame can be. It's almost magnetic. You can't look away. It breaks up the dark and allows for some visibility, increasingly so as you draw closer to the flame. If you've ever wandered around in the darkness, bumping into things and fearful of what else might be out there, you know how much relief and joy one small light can bring.

We live in a dark and broken world, and the world was dark and broken during John the Baptist's lifetime as well. John stood out because he was a bright light in the darkness. In a world characterized by division and distrust, he spoke of hope. He announced to everyone that the promised One had already arrived and was on His way, that humankind was so close to redemption. John the Baptist's sole purpose for living was to call attention to Jesus as the Messiah, to ensure people would be prepared and watching out for Him because they'd heard He was coming. John was just one small flame in comparison to who would be coming next.

Demonstrating Christ's love to others and testifying to the hope we have in Him allows us to burn brighter too. There are many ways to be a light in a dark world: bring someone a little peace, a little hope, a little strength, or a little love. The more you look to Jesus's example, the brighter your life will shine.

# WHERE ARE YOU?

*Why does the apostle John use the term "the light" to describe Jesus in the first chapter of his gospel?*

_____

_____

_____

_____

*When have you shared the light of Jesus with someone?*

_____

_____

_____

_____

*When you are confronted with anger or frustration, what actions can you take to "love like Jesus"?*

_____

_____

_____

_____

_____

# A PRAYER

Jesus, You are the Light of the World. Thank You for shining Your light into the darkness. I praise You that Your light has come into my heart and life. Help me to shine so others can see You. In Your name, amen.

# DAY 22:
## THE NOT-SO-OBVIOUS CHOICE

## SCRIPTURE READING

MATTHEW 3:1–12 (MSG)

*While Jesus was living in the Galilean hills, John, called "the Baptizer," was preaching in the desert country of Judea. His message was simple and austere, like his desert surroundings: "Change your life. God's kingdom is here."*

*John and his message were authorized by Isaiah's prophecy:*

> *Thunder in the desert!*
> *Prepare for God's arrival!*
> *Make the road smooth and straight!*

*John dressed in a camel-hair habit tied at the waist by a leather strap. He lived on a diet of locusts and wild field honey. People poured out of Jerusalem, Judea, and the Jordanian countryside to hear and see him in action. There at the Jordan River those who came to confess their sins were baptized into a changed life.*

*When John realized that a lot of Pharisees and Sadducees were showing up for a baptismal experience because it was becoming the popular thing to do, he exploded: "Brood of snakes! What do you think you're doing slithering down here to the river? Do you think a little water on your snakeskins is going to make any difference? It's your life that must change, not your skin! And don't think you can pull rank by claiming Abraham as father. Being a descendant of Abraham is neither here nor there. Descendants of Abraham are a dime a dozen. What counts is your life. Is it green and flourishing? Because if it's deadwood, it goes on the fire.*

*"I'm baptizing you here in the river, turning your old life in for a kingdom life. The real action comes next: The main character in this drama—compared to him I'm a mere stagehand—will ignite the kingdom life within you, a fire within you, the Holy Spirit within you, changing you from the inside out. He's going to clean house—make a clean sweep of your lives. He'll place everything true in its proper place before God; everything false he'll put out with the trash to be burned."*

SEE ALSO: MARK 1:1–8; LUKE 3:1–18

## LIFE LESSONS

John the Baptist probably seemed like a strange fellow to be announcing the coming of the Son of God. He certainly didn't look or act like other people. But John's existence, like Jesus's, was foretold. Some seven hundred years before the births of John and Jesus, Isaiah prophesied John's role in readying the world for Jesus's arrival, describing John as a voice shouting in the wilderness. (See Isaiah 40:1–9.)

God often doesn't pick the obvious choice to accomplish His will, and although John may have come across as a little odd, his passion for Christ's arrival was unrivaled. He preached with boldness and lived with an intense, single-minded purpose: "Prepare the way." And that he did. In fact, he did it so well that some people wanted to name him the Messiah. He was having none of that. Instead of taking any credit for himself, John continually turned people toward the coming Savior, promising that his baptism by water would pale when compared with the baptism by the Holy Spirit that was to come.

## WHERE ARE YOU?

*How would you describe John the Baptist? What do you think he was like?*

---
---
---
---
---

*Does John the Baptist remind you of anyone? If so, in what ways?*

---
---
---
---
---

*How would you summarize John's core message?*

_____

_____

_____

_____

_____

## A PRAYER

Jesus, I pray that You would prepare my heart for You, Your love, and the impending transformation of my life in Your hands, just as You prepared the hearts of so many others. Help me to live every day with a heart ready to see what You have in store. In Your name, amen.

# DAY 23:
## THE FATHER'S APPROVAL

## SCRIPTURE READING

MATTHEW 3:13–17 (MSG)

*Jesus then appeared, arriving at the Jordan River from Galilee. He wanted John to baptize him. John objected, "I'm the one who needs to be baptized, not you!"*

*But Jesus insisted. "Do it. God's work, putting things right all these centuries, is coming together right now in this baptism." So John did it.*

*The moment Jesus came up out of the baptismal waters, the skies opened up and he saw God's Spirit—it looked like a dove—descending and landing on him. And along with the Spirit, a voice: "This is my Son, chosen and marked by my love, delight of my life."*

SEE ALSO: MARK 1:9–11; LUKE 3:21–22

## LIFE LESSONS

Have you ever swelled with pride watching someone you love do something special? Sometimes in these moments we're swept away by an overwhelming desire to tell everyone about it so they, too, can affirm how special it is. I imagine that's how God felt as He watched His Son Jesus be baptized.

The *New International Version* translates God's words after the baptism as follows: *"This is my Son, whom I love; with him I am well pleased"* (Matthew 3:17). Whether we read God's statement as one of pleasure or joy, in this moment, we have a glimpse of the significant and heartfelt relationship between Father and Son.

Jesus didn't *need* to be baptized; He was already pure and free of sin. He did it as an act of obedience to God. And when Jesus emerged from the water after John baptized Him, God made it clear who Jesus was and to whom He belonged. God opened the heavens, an event that must have caught *everyone's* attention, to publicly announce His approval.

Here we read of a proud Father introducing His Son. This was His moment to tell everyone present, *This is He. He's here.* This moment cemented who Jesus was in the eyes of all who were present and revealed God's immense fatherly love.

## WHERE ARE YOU?

*Why did Jesus want to be baptized by John?*

_____

_____

_____

_____

*Think of a time someone told you they were proud of you. How did that make you feel?*

_____

_____

_____

_____

*Why is this example of God's fatherly love for Jesus significant?*

_____

_____

_____

_____

## A PRAYER

Father God, thank You for speaking Your approval of Jesus at His baptism so people would know that He was absolutely Your Son. Jesus, thank You for being obedient to Your heavenly Father and for giving us a perfect example to follow. Holy Spirit, thank You for coming down and demonstrating Your power as Jesus came up out of the water. In the name of the Father, Son, and Spirit, amen.

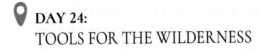

# DAY 24:
## TOOLS FOR THE WILDERNESS

## SCRIPTURE READING

MATTHEW 4:1–11 (MSG)

*Next Jesus was taken into the wild by the Spirit for the Test. The Devil was ready to give it. Jesus prepared for the Test by fasting forty days and forty nights. That left him, of course, in a state of extreme hunger, which the Devil took advantage of in the first test: "Since you are God's Son, speak the word that will turn these stones into loaves of bread."*

*Jesus answered by quoting Deuteronomy: "It takes more than bread to stay alive. It takes a steady stream of words from God's mouth."*

*For the second test the Devil took him to the Holy City. He sat him on top of the Temple and said, "Since you are God's Son, jump." The Devil goaded him by quoting Psalm 91: "He has placed you in the care of angels. They will catch you so that you won't so much as stub your toe on a stone."*

*Jesus countered with another citation from Deuteronomy: "Don't you dare test the Lord your God."*

*For the third test, the Devil took him to the peak of a huge mountain. He gestured expansively, pointing out all the earth's kingdoms, how glorious they all were. Then he said, "They're yours—lock, stock, and barrel. Just go down on your knees and worship me, and they're yours."*

*Jesus's refusal was curt: "Beat it, Satan!" He backed his rebuke with a third quotation from Deuteronomy: "Worship the Lord your God, and only him. Serve him with absolute single-heartedness."*

*The Test was over. The Devil left. And in his place, angels! Angels came and took care of Jesus's needs.*

SEE ALSO: MARK 1:12–13; LUKE 4:1–13

## LIFE LESSONS

A spiritual high, followed immediately by a lonely trek into the wilderness without food, temptation His only companion? That would have been quite the comedown for Jesus following His hearing the pleased affirmation of His

Father and having the Holy Spirit descend on Him like a dove. But while He was struggling, Jesus held fast to what He knew, what He carried with Him always: God's Word and God's promises.

Jesus resisted hunger and temptation by quoting Scripture. He knew what God's promises said and what God wanted, so He used those as beacons to follow when everything else became difficult, when He was most likely at the end of His rope.

Jesus had invested time studying God's Word so He would be ready for whatever came His way and would have something to hold on to when circumstances seemed bleak or unfair. Jesus entered the wilderness full of the Spirit and left the wilderness in the *power* of the Spirit.

What do you do when you're facing adversity? We all experience some extreme ups and downs. It's easy to give in or give up when we have nothing to hold on to, no clear direction. Quitting feels easiest when we're trying to find it solely in ourselves to keep going. Jesus knows the despair of our lows, and He knows the potential of our strength even when we can't see it. Praise God that He has provided tools, such as Scripture, to help us in those low times.

## WHERE ARE YOU?

*Who are your go-to people to help you when you face adversity?*

_____

_____

_____

_____

_____

*Do you have any go-to Scriptures to encourage yourself when you experience hard times?*

_____

_____

_____

_____

_____

*What has sustained you when you have faced difficulty or despair?*

---

---

---

---

---

## A PRAYER

Jesus, thank You for the power of Your Word to protect and guide me when I'm going through hard times and faced with hard decisions. Help me to prioritize studying the Bible so I can know You better. In Your name, amen.

# DAY 25:
## THE PERFECT LAMB

## SCRIPTURE READING

### JOHN 1:19–34 (NLT)

*This was John's testimony when the Jewish leaders sent priests and Temple assistants from Jerusalem to ask John, "Who are you?" He came right out and said, "I am not the Messiah."*

*"Well then, who are you?" they asked. "Are you Elijah?"*

*"No," he replied.*

*"Are you the Prophet we are expecting?"*

*"No."*

*"Then who are you? We need an answer for those who sent us. What do you have to say about yourself?"*

*John replied in the words of the prophet Isaiah:*

> *"I am a voice shouting in the wilderness,*
>
> > *'Clear the way for the LORD's coming!'"*

*Then the Pharisees who had been sent asked him, "If you aren't the Messiah or Elijah or the Prophet, what right do you have to baptize?"*

*John told them, "I baptize with water, but right here in the crowd is someone you do not recognize. Though his ministry follows mine, I'm not even worthy to be his slave and untie the straps of his sandal." This encounter took place in Bethany, an area east of the Jordan River, where John was baptizing.*

*The next day John saw Jesus coming toward him and said, "Look! The Lamb of God who takes away the sin of the world! He is the one I was talking about when I said, 'A man is coming after me who is far greater than I am, for he existed long before me.' I did not recognize him as the Messiah, but I have been baptizing with water so that he might be revealed to Israel."*

*Then John testified, "I saw the Holy Spirit descending like a dove from heaven and resting upon him. I didn't know he was the one, but when God sent me to baptize with water, he told me, 'The one on whom you see the Spirit descend and rest is the one who will baptize with the Holy Spirit.' I saw this happen to Jesus, so I testify that he is the Chosen One of God."*

## LIFE LESSONS

John the Baptist spoke bluntly about the distinctions between himself and Jesus, making it clear that they were in no way the same. John is the preparer, and Jesus is the Messiah. John knew his part in all this. And, here, he made Jesus's identity absolutely clear.

Upon seeing Jesus, John declared, *"Look! The Lamb of God who takes away the sin of the world!"* (John 1:29 NLT). With this declaration, John evoked the concept of sacrifice. Eighty-five of the ninety-six references to a lamb in the Old Testament use the term in connection with a sacrifice. In biblical times, people would bring a lamb to the temple to be sacrificed as a sin offering. The priest would inspect the lamb beforehand to ensure it was without spot or blemish. John's identification of Jesus as the "Lamb of God" signaled that this Person was perfect, without blemish. He identified Jesus as the perfect offering for the world, sent straight from God to cleanse everyone's sin—to redeem *all* people.

In our culture, the image of a lamb being sacrificed seems cruel and barbaric. But if we are going to truly understand why Jesus lived and why He sacrificed Himself for us, we have to understand what He endured. We need to realize that Jesus, though He is the Son of God, experienced unspeakable pain and horrific cruelty for us after leading a life of perfection. Reflecting on His sacrifice should make us fall on our knees in gratitude and worship.

## WHERE ARE YOU?

*The Pharisees asked John the Baptist, "Who are you?" If you were asked that question, how would you answer?*

*What did John the Baptist declare about Jesus?*

_____

_____

_____

_____

_____

*When have the words of another person profoundly affected your life?*

_____

_____

_____

_____

_____

## A PRAYER

Jesus, thank You for offering Your life as the only perfect sacrifice that would provide forgiveness for my sins. Thank You for paying my debt in full. I am forever grateful for Your sacrifice. In Your name, amen.

# DAY 26:
## LIVING A LIFE OF PURPOSE

## SCRIPTURE READING

### JOHN 1:35–42 (NIV)

*The next day John was there again with two of his disciples. When he saw Jesus passing by, he said, "Look, the Lamb of God!"*

*When the two disciples heard him say this, they followed Jesus. Turning around, Jesus saw them following and asked, "What do you want?"*

*They said, "Rabbi" (which means "Teacher"), "where are you staying?"*

*"Come," he replied, "and you will see."*

*So they went and saw where he was staying, and they spent that day with him. It was about four in the afternoon.*

*Andrew, Simon Peter's brother, was one of the two who heard what John had said and who had followed Jesus. The first thing Andrew did was to find his brother Simon and tell him, "We have found the Messiah" (that is, the Christ). And he brought him to Jesus.*

*Jesus looked at him and said, "You are Simon son of John. You will be called Cephas" (which, when translated, is Peter).*

## LIFE LESSONS

The hope of better things and the desire to live a purposeful life—these two yearnings drive people to search, to put themselves out there. They open minds and hearts, preparing people for change.

When two followers of John the Baptist heard him identify Jesus as the Lamb of God for the second time in two days, they were ready to give up everything and follow Jesus. In fact, they were so ready that one of them, Andrew, immediately ran to his brother to share the word and invite him along. Andrew's actions give us a blueprint of how to share our own good news: Just go and do it. Invite others. Express your excitement.

These men's hearts and minds were already open, so they *could* throw themselves into the fray at the announcement that their Savior had arrived. They had already been searching for something better, something with purpose—so when they found it, they were ready to act. We, too, must pursue a life lived with purpose and be ready for change. New opportunities may be right around the corner. We must keep our hearts open to God's movement and share the good news of Jesus with those around us as we walk with our Savior. We just might inspire someone to come along with us on our journey, as Andrew did.

## WHERE ARE YOU?

*What is the most important news you've ever shared with someone?*

_____

_____

_____

_____

_____

*When have you been invited to "come and see" something interesting, amazing, or wonderful?*

_____

_____

_____

_____

_____

*In your own words, what were the disciples in this passage looking for?*

_____

_____

_____

_____

_____

## A PRAYER

God, thank You for sending John the Baptist to boldly identify Your Son, the Lamb of God. Thank You for his boldness to declare Your name and share the good news with those around him. I pray for an open heart to continue seeking more of You and the life You offer. In Jesus's name, amen.

# DAY 27:
## MEETING US WHERE WE ARE

## SCRIPTURE READING

JOHN 1:43–51 (NIV)

*The next day Jesus decided to leave for Galilee. Finding Philip, he said to him, "Follow me."*

*Philip, like Andrew and Peter, was from the town of Bethsaida. Philip found Nathanael and told him, "We have found the one Moses wrote about in the Law, and about whom the prophets also wrote—Jesus of Nazareth, the son of Joseph."*

*"Nazareth! Can anything good come from there?" Nathanael asked.*

*"Come and see," said Philip.*

*When Jesus saw Nathanael approaching, he said of him, "Here truly is an Israelite in whom there is no deceit."*

*"How do you know me?" Nathanael asked.*

*Jesus answered, "I saw you while you were still under the fig tree before Philip called you."*

*Then Nathanael declared, "Rabbi, you are the Son of God; you are the king of Israel."*

*Jesus said, "You believe because I told you I saw you under the fig tree. You will see greater things than that." He then added, "Very truly I tell you, you will see 'heaven open, and the angels of God ascending and descending on' the Son of Man."*

## LIFE LESSONS

All of us have moments of skepticism. Doubt is one way of protecting ourselves. And, whether we recognize it or not, we all carry prejudice from our experiences and upbringing into our interactions. Nathanael was no different. When he heard that Jesus had come from Nazareth, he immediately dismissed Him. *"Nazareth! Can anything good come from there?"* (John 1:46 NIV). What a human reaction!

Jesus knew Nathanael had scoffed at the idea of His being the Messiah, but He used that as a connection point instead of writing him off. Jesus leaned into the relationship when many of us would have cut our losses and moved on. Only after Jesus told Nathanael things about himself that nobody else could have known did Nathanael begin to believe.

Jesus meets you where you are. He knows exactly who you are, where you come from, and how you ended up where you are now. He has compassion and understanding for your circumstances. He wants to help you overcome your doubts because He has a purpose for your life. You just have to *let* Him meet with you.

## WHERE ARE YOU?

*How do you tend to react to new voices or new ideas?*

*What do you remember about your first encounter with Jesus?*

*In a world full of news—some of it fake news—how do you discern what is true?*

## A PRAYER

Lord Jesus, thank You for Your grace. You know everything about me—my strengths and my shortcomings—and You still want to meet me where I am. You still have a purpose and a plan for my life. Help me to glorify You as I follow You daily. In Your name, amen.

# A PRIVATE MIRACLE

## SCRIPTURE READING

JOHN 2:1–12 (NLT)

*The next day there was a wedding celebration in the village of Cana in Galilee. Jesus's mother was there, and Jesus and his disciples were also invited to the celebration. The wine supply ran out during the festivities, so Jesus's mother told him, "They have no more wine."*

*"Dear woman, that's not our problem," Jesus replied. "My time has not yet come."*

*But his mother told the servants, "Do whatever he tells you."*

*Standing nearby were six stone water jars, used for Jewish ceremonial washing. Each could hold twenty to thirty gallons. Jesus told the servants, "Fill the jars with water."*

*When the jars had been filled, he said, "Now dip some out, and take it to the master of ceremonies." So the servants followed his instructions.*

*When the master of ceremonies tasted the water that was now wine, not knowing where it had come from (though, of course, the servants knew), he called the bridegroom over. "A host always serves the best wine first," he said. "Then, when everyone has had a lot to drink, he brings out the less expensive wine. But you have kept the best until now!"*

*This miraculous sign at Cana in Galilee was the first time Jesus revealed his glory. And his disciples believed in him.*

*After the wedding he went to Capernaum for a few days with his mother, his brothers, and his disciples.*

## LIFE LESSONS

When Mary calls Jesus to help at a wedding they're attending, He is reluctant. He doesn't want to call attention to Himself yet, to perform miracles and cause a spectacle in the middle of this celebration with so many people present. Mary comes to Him regardless, knowing His love for people will compel Him to act.

In the Jewish culture of Jesus's day, running out of wine was a breach of good hospitality that would have brought shame to the newlyweds. Mary shows faith in Jesus's heart for others and faith in His ability to do something about it. She knows He can and will perform a miracle—His first recorded in Scripture.

Jesus, moved by compassion, performs the miracle, but He does so quietly. Only the disciples and the servants witness His power. Jesus's miracle doesn't overshadow the festivities; He ensures the guests can remain focused on the bride and groom. At the same time, His actions establish His power in front of His disciples, those closest to Him. This miracle shows Jesus's authority over nature: He is able to transform basic elements—an incredible power.

Mary believed without a doubt that Jesus would help the couple. She believed in His power before she'd fully seen it. Jesus does not withhold when we reach out to Him in faith. He truly loves us and will respond to our needs, though maybe not in the way we expect.

## WHERE ARE YOU?

*In your view, what is the significance of this miracle being performed only for the servants and the disciples to see?*

*Why do you think the location of Jesus's first miracle—a marriage celebration—is significant?*

*How does this passage reveal both the humanity and the divinity of Jesus?*

_____

_____

_____

_____

_____

## A PRAYER

Jesus, thank You for Your endless compassion for me. We know You show up at all moments—large and small—for our journey. Help me to have that faith and certainty. May I trust and obey You even when it doesn't make sense. In Your name, amen.

## DAY 29:
## THE CELEBRATION OF PASSOVER

## SCRIPTURE READING

JOHN 2:13 (NIV)

*When it was almost time for the Jewish Passover, Jesus went up to Jerusalem.*

## LIFE LESSONS

The first Passover took place over a thousand years before Jesus's birth when God delivered His people from slavery through a series of plagues that culminated with the angel of death visiting the region. God had instructed His people to sprinkle the blood of a sacrificial lamb on the doorposts of their homes to ensure the angel of death would pass over those homes and let them be. The Israelites followed God's instructions. Their firstborn sons were spared—but the Egyptians' were not. It was this final plague that led Pharaoh to release God's people, freeing them from slavery.

The Israelites commemorated this monumental event every year—and Jewish people continue to observe it today. Year after year, the people of Israel never forget to stop and celebrate God's miracle of delivering them from enslavement and giving them freedom. May we never stop celebrating all that God does along our journeys and the miracle of our own freedom in Christ.

## WHERE ARE YOU?

*What family or cultural rituals do you celebrate?*

*How do you celebrate the important moments in your life?*

_____

_____

_____

_____

_____

*In what ways do you remember and celebrate God's presence in your life?*

_____

_____

_____

_____

_____

## A PRAYER

Jesus, thank You for the opportunity to remember all that You have done. As I am reminded of Your goodness, I rejoice in the riches of Your grace. I am overwhelmed with gratitude. I love You, Lord. In Your name, amen.

# DAY 30:
# OUR NATURE, HIS NATURE

## SCRIPTURE READING

JOHN 2:14–25 (NLT)

*In the Temple area he saw merchants selling cattle, sheep, and doves for sacrifices; he also saw dealers at tables exchanging foreign money. Jesus made a whip from some ropes and chased them all out of the Temple. He drove out the sheep and cattle, scattered the money changers' coins over the floor, and turned over their tables. Then, going over to the people who sold doves, he told them, "Get these things out of here. Stop turning my Father's house into a marketplace!"*

*Then his disciples remembered this prophecy from the Scriptures: "Passion for God's house will consume me."*

*But the Jewish leaders demanded, "What are you doing? If God gave you authority to do this, show us a miraculous sign to prove it."*

*"All right," Jesus replied. "Destroy this temple, and in three days I will raise it up."*

*"What!" they exclaimed. "It has taken forty-six years to build this Temple, and you can rebuild it in three days?" But when Jesus said "this temple," he meant his own body. After he was raised from the dead, his disciples remembered he had said this, and they believed both the Scriptures and what Jesus had said.*

*Because of the miraculous signs Jesus did in Jerusalem at the Passover celebration, many began to trust in him. But Jesus didn't trust them, because he knew all about people. No one needed to tell him about human nature, for he knew what was in each person's heart.*

## LIFE LESSONS

Human nature is an often-discussed topic around the globe. The propensity for greed and the tendency to twist pure things for the purpose of our personal benefit resides in everyone. Here the temple had been built to magnify God, but people had turned it into anything *but* a place of worship. Humans converted something meant to be pure and holy into an immoral marketplace.

Jesus loved His Father so much, He couldn't bear to see the temple like that— perverted into sales ploys and sucking the last pennies from people on their way to seek God. He was so frustrated and offended that He chased the merchants and dealers out. These actions were the first spark of the controversy that ultimately led to His future as the Temple destroyed and rebuilt.

And although people had begun to trust that Jesus was who He said He was, He knew He couldn't trust them back. This doesn't mean He didn't love them. It means He knew what they were capable of, what they were still doing, how they refused to change. He knew the many, many failings of human beings, but He was still willing to give His life for all of us. His passion to set things right, to return them to what they are meant to be, is in His nature. He desires for us to be who we are meant to be in God.

## WHERE ARE YOU?

*In your own words, why was Jesus angry at the people selling in the temple?*

_____

_____

_____

_____

_____

*What were the different responses to Jesus's words and actions in this passage?*

_____

_____

_____

_____

_____

*Why was it important that Jesus predicted His death and resurrection?*

_____

_____

_____

_____

_____

## A PRAYER

Lord Jesus, thank You for continuing to love us and believe in us despite our broken human nature, despite our failings. Thank You for Your passion and Your love for Your Father, the church, and every human being, no matter our history or where we are in life. In Your name, amen.

# DAY 31:
## EAGER TO ANSWER

## SCRIPTURE READING

JOHN 3:1–21 (NIV)

*Now there was a Pharisee, a man named Nicodemus who was a member of the Jewish ruling council. He came to Jesus at night and said, "Rabbi, we know that you are a teacher who has come from God. For no one could perform the signs you are doing if God were not with him."*

*Jesus replied, "Very truly I tell you, no one can see the kingdom of God unless they are born again."*

*"How can someone be born when they are old?" Nicodemus asked. "Surely they cannot enter a second time into their mother's womb to be born!"*

*Jesus answered, "Very truly I tell you, no one can enter the kingdom of God unless they are born of water and the Spirit. Flesh gives birth to flesh, but the Spirit gives birth to spirit. You should not be surprised at my saying, 'You must be born again.' The wind blows wherever it pleases. You hear its sound, but you cannot tell where it comes from or where it is going. So it is with everyone born of the Spirit."*

*"How can this be?" Nicodemus asked.*

*"You are Israel's teacher," said Jesus, "and do you not understand these things? Very truly I tell you, we speak of what we know, and we testify to what we have seen, but still you people do not accept our testimony. I have spoken to you of earthly things and you do not believe; how then will you believe if I speak of heavenly things? No one has ever gone into heaven except the one who came from heaven—the Son of Man. Just as Moses lifted up the snake in the wilderness, so the Son of Man must be lifted up, that everyone who believes may have eternal life in him."*

*For God so loved the world that he gave his one and only Son, that whoever believes in him shall not perish but have eternal life. For God did not send his Son into the world to condemn the world, but to save the world through him. Whoever believes in him is not condemned, but whoever does not believe stands condemned already because they have not believed in the name of God's one and only Son. This is the verdict: Light has come into the world, but people loved darkness instead of light because their deeds were evil. Everyone who does evil hates the light, and will not come into the light for fear that their deeds will be exposed. But whoever lives by the truth comes into the light, so that it may be seen plainly that what they have done has been done in the sight of God.*

## LIFE LESSONS

Jesus's exchange with Nicodemus might seem like a series of misunderstandings. Yet through this conversation, Jesus shared one of the greatest truths we have in Scripture: the reality of how much God really loves us.

God loves us so much that He gave all He had. He gave Himself. And not just for one person but for the whole world. Not just for those who knew Jesus at that time but for all of us who know Him now, and for those yet to know Him.

Just as Jesus answered Nicodemus's questions, He is eager to answer ours. Although we may not always get the answer we want, we will always receive the one we need.

## WHERE ARE YOU?

*Why did Nicodemus have to come to Jesus at night?*

_____

_____

_____

_____

*When do you find it easiest to talk to Jesus? When do you find it the most difficult to do so?*

_____

_____

_____

_____

_____

*If you could ask Jesus one question, what would it be?*

_____

_____

_____

_____

## A PREAYER

Jesus, I pray for acceptance and understanding for the days when Your answers aren't what I want to hear. Thank You for loving us so much that You gave Your life for us, and thank You for bringing Your light into this world. In Your name, amen.

# DAY 32:
## LESS OF US AND MORE OF HIM

## SCRIPTURE READING

### JOHN 3:22–36 (NLT)

*Then Jesus and his disciples left Jerusalem and went into the Judean countryside. Jesus spent some time with them there, baptizing people.*

*At this time John the Baptist was baptizing at Aenon, near Salim, because there was plenty of water there; and people kept coming to him for baptism. (This was before John was thrown into prison.) A debate broke out between John's disciples and a certain Jew over ceremonial cleansing. So John's disciples came to him and said, "Rabbi, the man you met on the other side of the Jordan River, the one you identified as the Messiah, is also baptizing people. And everybody is going to him instead of coming to us."*

*John replied, "No one can receive anything unless God gives it from heaven. You yourselves know how plainly I told you, 'I am not the Messiah. I am only here to prepare the way for him.' It is the bridegroom who marries the bride, and the bridegroom's friend is simply glad to stand with him and hear his vows. Therefore, I am filled with joy at his success. He must become greater and greater, and I must become less and less.*

*"He has come from above and is greater than anyone else. We are of the earth, and we speak of earthly things, but he has come from heaven and is greater than anyone else. He testifies about what he has seen and heard, but how few believe what he tells them! Anyone who accepts his testimony can affirm that God is true. For he is sent by God. He speaks God's words, for God gives him the Spirit without limit. The Father loves his Son and has put everything into his hands. And anyone who believes in God's Son has eternal life. Anyone who doesn't obey the Son will never experience eternal life but remains under God's angry judgment."*

## LIFE LESSONS

For many of us, it can be hard to let go of the spotlight once we've secured it. Once things get going, it's easy to forget how or why we started and who helped us along the way. In a world where we compete for followers on social media, we can imagine what it's like to lose followers. More difficult is imagining intentionally instructing our followers to follow someone else, especially after all the work and time we've put in toward earning their loyalty. Yet that's just what John the Baptist does in this passage.

John the Baptist had many followers. He was essentially a sold-out success as a forerunner for the coming Messiah. At the same time, he knew his place, and he never forgot why he was doing the work he did. John wanted *everyone* to move toward Jesus. And he kept that end goal in sight. When other people tried to create discord by saying Jesus was baptizing more people, John was unperturbed. His unselfish nature kept him from accepting personal praise or participating in petty jealousy. Instead, he stayed steady and pointed to Jesus, reminding others that Jesus was the whole reason John was there doing what he was doing.

John compared his relationship with Jesus to that of a groomsman standing next to the groom. Jesus, of course, was the groom, and His church was the bride. John's purpose was to support and aid in any way he could to ensure the two came together successfully. This selfless attitude is reflected in his words in John 3:30: *"He must become greater and greater, and I must become less and less"* (NLT).

John's stature in relation to Jesus is a model for our own faith journeys. As we let Jesus become more and more in our lives, we'll find that our own self-seeking and otherwise destructive behaviors become less and less.

## WHERE ARE YOU?

*When have you had to play a role you were not comfortable with?*

*Did any insecurities factor into your discomfort? If so, in what way?*

_____
_____
_____
_____
_____

*In this passage, what stands out to you about John the Baptist?*

_____
_____
_____
_____
_____

## A PRAYER

Thank You, Jesus, for the humility of John the Baptist. Let me be just as humble in my walk with You. I pray for more of You in my life. Help me to always remember what my purpose is and to live this life with that in mind. In Your name, amen.

RECEIVE OR REJECT?

## SCRIPTURE READING

LUKE 3:19–20 (NIV)

*But when John rebuked Herod the tetrarch because of his marriage to Herodias, his brother's wife, and all the other evil things he had done, Herod added this to them all: He locked John up in prison.*

## LIFE LESSONS

John the Baptist wasn't afraid to tell the truth. He preached the same message of repentance regardless of his audience. His boldness eventually brought about his imprisonment: he called out King Herod not just for marrying his brother's wife, but also for many acts of immorality and brutality.

John's message did not fall on deaf ears. And those who hated the message immediately turned on the messenger.

When we are confronted with our own shortcomings, we have two choices. We can receive the message with an open heart, ask for forgiveness, and change; or, we can reject the message and continue lying to ourselves and seeking the company of those who will enable us. Fortunately, neither of these two options usually results in life or death, freedom or imprisonment. However, by rejecting those who call us out when we are wrong, we choose to be like Herod: we hurt other people through our recklessness and remain bound to our decisions and the circumstances surrounding them.

## WHERE ARE YOU?

*Have you ever invited anyone to help hold you accountable for your actions? If so, how did it go?*

_____

_____

_____

_____

_____

*When have you been angry with someone for calling you out in some way?*

_____

_____

_____

_____

_____

*In a world where people are easily offended, how can we practice accountability?*

_____

_____

_____

_____

_____

## A PRAYER

Jesus, help me to receive Your Word with a humble spirit and an open heart. When I am wrong, give me the wisdom to listen and the humility to ask for forgiveness. When others confront me about my shortcomings, help me to look for the truth and respond appropriately. In Your name, amen.

# DAY 34:
## BRINGING DOWN BARRIERS

## SCRIPTURE READING

JOHN 4:1–26 (NLT)

*Jesus knew the Pharisees had heard that he was baptizing and making more disciples than John (though Jesus himself didn't baptize them—his disciples did). So he left Judea and returned to Galilee.*

*He had to go through Samaria on the way. Eventually he came to the Samaritan village of Sychar, near the field that Jacob gave to his son Joseph. Jacob's well was there; and Jesus, tired from the long walk, sat wearily beside the well about noontime. Soon a Samaritan woman came to draw water, and Jesus said to her, "Please give me a drink." He was alone at the time because his disciples had gone into the village to buy some food.*

*The woman was surprised, for Jews refuse to have anything to do with Samaritans. She said to Jesus, "You are a Jew, and I am a Samaritan woman. Why are you asking me for a drink?"*

*Jesus replied, "If you only knew the gift God has for you and who you are speaking to, you would ask me, and I would give you living water."*

*"But sir, you don't have a rope or a bucket," she said, "and this well is very deep. Where would you get this living water? And besides, do you think you're greater than our ancestor Jacob, who gave us this well? How can you offer better water than he and his sons and his animals enjoyed?"*

*Jesus replied, "Anyone who drinks this water will soon become thirsty again. But those who drink the water I give will never be thirsty again. It becomes a fresh, bubbling spring within them, giving them eternal life."*

*"Please, sir," the woman said, "give me this water! Then I'll never be thirsty again, and I won't have to come here to get water."*

*"Go and get your husband," Jesus told her.*

*"I don't have a husband," the woman replied.*

*Jesus said, "You're right! You don't have a husband—for you have had five husbands, and you aren't even married to the man you're living with now. You certainly spoke the truth!"*

"Sir," the woman said, "you must be a prophet. So tell me, why is it that you Jews insist that Jerusalem is the only place of worship, while we Samaritans claim it is here at Mount Gerizim, where our ancestors worshiped?"

Jesus replied, "Believe me, dear woman, the time is coming when it will no longer matter whether you worship the Father on this mountain or in Jerusalem. You Samaritans know very little about the one you worship, while we Jews know all about him, for salvation comes through the Jews. But the time is coming—indeed it's here now—when true worshipers will worship the Father in spirit and in truth. The Father is looking for those who will worship him that way. For God is Spirit, so those who worship him must worship in spirit and in truth."

The woman said, "I know the Messiah is coming—the one who is called Christ. When he comes, he will explain everything to us."

Then Jesus told her, "I AM the Messiah!"

## LIFE LESSONS

Sometimes when we're trying to communicate with another person, it can feel like major differences are standing between us, making it impossible to reach a point of mutual understanding. Often those differences make things so tense we just give up. In some circumstances, we don't even want the wall to come down.

Jesus broke down barriers as He conversed with this Samaritan woman and helped her understand that God's love doesn't discriminate and that His redemption would be for all people. Religious preferences wouldn't matter. A shameful history wouldn't matter. Gender, social status, race—they would make no difference. Jesus dismantled every gatekeeping thought this woman could come up with—obstacles like, "I am not like you," "We don't worship the same," "We are socially different." These things didn't matter to Jesus.

If Jesus is for all people, we too should be for all people. We can overcome the barriers in our relationships by reaching out and accepting others as they are. It can be uncomfortable, but you have to start somewhere. Begin by recognizing that all people are your fellow human beings just trying to get through life. Make that initial contact. Talk to them.

You can't overcome anything if you don't take the first step. Keep an open mind as you interact with others. Not everyone will be receptive, but you might be surprised. Being like Jesus means accepting people as they are and not letting your differences be a barrier to His love and kindness.

## WHERE ARE YOU?

*How would you describe Jesus's response to the Samaritan woman?*

_____

_____

_____

_____

_____

*What barriers hold you back from forming relationships with those who are different from you?*

_____

_____

_____

_____

_____

*If you were to truly love others like Jesus, what in your life would need to change?*

_____

_____

_____

_____

_____

## A PRAYER

Thank You, Jesus, for breaking down barriers. Thank You for talking to someone broken like me. Help me to be different, to be kind, and to refuse to let barriers keep me from treating others as they should be treated. I trust in Your power to break down walls. Use me to demonstrate Your love and acceptance. In Your name, amen.

# DAY 35:
## NOURISHING THE BODY *AND* THE SOUL

## SCRIPTURE READING

JOHN 4:27–38 (NIV)

*Just then his disciples returned and were surprised to find him talking with a woman. But no one asked, "What do you want?" or "Why are you talking with her?"*

*Then, leaving her water jar, the woman went back to the town and said to the people, "Come, see a man who told me everything I ever did. Could this be the Messiah?" They came out of the town and made their way toward him.*

*Meanwhile his disciples urged him, "Rabbi, eat something."*

*But he said to them, "I have food to eat that you know nothing about."*

*Then his disciples said to each other, "Could someone have brought him food?"*

*"My food," said Jesus, "is to do the will of him who sent me and to finish his work. Don't you have a saying, 'It's still four months until harvest'? I tell you, open your eyes and look at the fields! They are ripe for harvest. Even now the one who reaps draws a wage and harvests a crop for eternal life, so that the sower and the reaper may be glad together. Thus the saying 'One sows and another reaps' is true. I sent you to reap what you have not worked for. Others have done the hard work, and you have reaped the benefits of their labor."*

## LIFE LESSONS

Have you ever been so excited, so overcome with emotion, that you dropped everything to tell others about it? John tells us that's what the Samaritan woman did after her conversation with Jesus. He says she left her water jar behind in her excitement to tell her fellow townspeople about Jesus. This was a big deal in her day. Her water jar was essential in helping provide for her daily needs. Like all of us, she *needed* water to live. Her encounter with Jesus, though, overrode her most basic priorities. She was so excited, she forgot about her physical needs and raced to tell everyone about the well that would never run dry.

After she had gone, Jesus's disciples urged Jesus to eat. In His response, we again see physical nourishment directly compared to the nourishment of the soul that comes from following Jesus. He chides His disciples by saying, in essence, "My food is to do the will of Him who sent me to do His work."

We can't survive without water and food, and we can't thrive without Jesus. Having Him in our lives is vital to nourishing our souls.

## WHERE ARE YOU?

*What is your favorite food? Is your response based purely on taste or on other factors, such as a fond memory or a positive association?*

_____

_____

_____

_____

_____

*In your own words, what is Jesus's message to His disciples in this passage?*

_____

_____

_____

_____

*If you were going to be more consistent in seeking Jesus daily, what change(s) would you need to make to your routine and/or your perspective?*

_____

_____

_____

_____

## A PRAYER

Jesus, thank You for nourishing my soul so I can thrive. I recognize that putting aside space and time for You is essential for my spiritual health. Help me to use Your lessons to the Samaritan woman and the disciples as reminders to set aside that time for You. In Your name, amen.

# DAY 36:
## JOY TO SHARE

## SCRIPTURE READING

JOHN 4:39–42 (NLT)

*Many Samaritans from the village believed in Jesus because the woman had said, "He told me everything I ever did!" When they came out to see him, they begged him to stay in their village. So he stayed for two days, long enough for many more to hear his message and believe. Then they said to the woman, "Now we believe, not just because of what you told us, but because we have heard him ourselves. Now we know that he is indeed the Savior of the world."*

## LIFE LESSONS

One single encounter, and the Samaritan woman couldn't stop talking about Jesus. She couldn't resist making sure everyone she knew (and probably several strangers as well) heard that she had met this extraordinary Man. Her excitement was infectious. Sharing her story led others to seek Him out—enough that Jesus spent a couple extra days in her village.

When we tell friends and family how Christ changes and improves our lives, we become like the Samaritan woman. If Jesus is doing something great in your life, share your joy. The world needs to experience that hope. If we feel embarrassed or reluctant to share our story, we might deprive someone of the opportunity to form their own relationship with God.

Perhaps Jesus has helped you to find peace about a situation, mend a relationship, or overcome an addiction. However He has worked in your life, tell others about it. Share your emotions, share your wins, share your comfort, and share your optimism. This sharing of the joy that we find as we walk with Jesus is the most powerful force in spreading the good news.

## WHERE ARE YOU?

*Have you ever shared your personal faith story with anybody? If so, who? What was the experience like?*

_____

_____

_____

_____

_____

*Why are we sometimes reluctant to share our faith with others?*

_____

_____

_____

_____

*In what ways does sharing our beliefs with someone have the potential to change our relationship with them?*

_____

_____

_____

_____

## A PRAYER

Jesus, thank You for the good things You've brought into my life. You've given me so many reasons to be joyful. Give me the courage to share Your love with those I meet. Help me to be a good communicator so I can make real connections and a genuine difference. In Your name, amen.

# DAY 37:
## SMALL GESTURES OF HOSPITALITY

## SCRIPTURE READING

JOHN 4:43–45 (NIV)

*After the two days he left for Galilee. (Now Jesus himself had pointed out that a prophet has no honor in his own country.) When he arrived in Galilee, the Galileans welcomed him. They had seen all that he had done in Jerusalem at the Passover Festival, for they also had been there.*

SEE ALSO: MARK 1:14–15; LUKE 4:14–15

## LIFE LESSONS

In the ancient Near East, hospitality was more than offering someone a beverage when they entered your home. It consisted of sacred codes of conduct. The region's desert environment made for harsh traveling conditions. For a traveler in biblical times, access to food and water was a matter of life and death. Consequently, a tradition arose requiring occupants of a city to welcome and care for any guests who arrived.

Cultural customs in our towns might not resemble those of Jesus's day, but that doesn't mean we can't embrace a habit of hospitality as we interact with people. Sometimes we can show the hospitality of Jesus in a big way by giving our time or our resources to help those in need. But *most* of our hospitality will come down to loving others as Jesus did. This involves simple acts like asking someone who is lonely to share a cup of coffee, making room for someone at a table, or asking a cashier how their day is going.

Smiles and kind words are a valuable currency in building up God's people. Each of us is equipped with unique means of showing hospitality to others and making them feel welcome and cared for.

## WHERE ARE YOU?

*Why do you suppose Jesus said that "a prophet has no honor in his own country" (John 4:44)?*

_____

_____

_____

_____

*Think of a memorable time when you extended hospitality to someone. What made that experience memorable?*

_____

_____

_____

_____

*In very practical ways, what does it look like when someone loves like Jesus?*

_____

_____

_____

_____

_____

## A PRAYER

Lord Jesus, thank You for showing Your hospitality to me first. Help me to be just as accommodating and also to recognize the needs of those around me. May I utilize the journey You have blessed me with to welcome others in Your name. I pray that my actions would reveal Your love in a way that welcomes people to You. In Your name, amen.

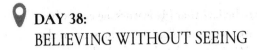

# DAY 38:
## BELIEVING WITHOUT SEEING

## SCRIPTURE READING

### JOHN 4:46–54 (NIV)

*Once more he visited Cana in Galilee, where he had turned the water into wine. And there was a certain royal official whose son lay sick at Capernaum. When this man heard that Jesus had arrived in Galilee from Judea, he went to him and begged him to come and heal his son, who was close to death.*

*"Unless you people see signs and wonders," Jesus told him, "you will never believe."*

*The royal official said, "Sir, come down before my child dies."*

*"Go," Jesus replied, "your son will live."*

*The man took Jesus at his word and departed. While he was still on the way, his servants met him with the news that his boy was living. When he inquired as to the time when his son got better, they said to him, "Yesterday, at one in the afternoon, the fever left him."*

*Then the father realized that this was the exact time at which Jesus had said to him, "Your son will live." So he and his whole household believed.*

*This was the second sign Jesus performed after coming from Judea to Galilee.*

## LIFE LESSONS

The phrase "seeing is believing" is common for a reason. It's easiest to trust what we can perceive with our own two eyes.

The royal official in this passage was desperate to bring Jesus to his house before his son died—but Jesus sent him back alone with only the promise that his boy would live. Jesus didn't need to be present to heal. His power was greater than that. All He wanted in return was faith—in this case, large faith: faith in what the man couldn't see.

Jesus's words weren't much for the man to grab hold of, but he believed anyway, right away. And the second he believed, his son's health at home began to improve. When the man realized this and told others about it, the people around him began to believe.

Jesus asks us to have faith. He asks us to believe that He is working even when we can't see the changes. He doesn't need a grand stage or to show up in the flesh to perform miracles in our lives. We just need to have faith that they're going to happen—and then the people around us may begin to believe as well.

## WHERE ARE YOU?

*How would you describe the faith of the father in this passage?*

_____

_____

_____

_____

_____

*Have you ever witnessed something that you considered to be miraculous? What occurred in that circumstance?*

_____

_____

_____

_____

*When has the Lord answered a prayer of yours in a way that was surprising, immediate, or obvious?*

_____

_____

_____

_____

## A PRAYER

Jesus, thank You for this incredible example of true faith. Sometimes You work in small or slow ways. Help me to have faith that You are working even when I can't see it. In Your name, amen.

## SCRIPTURE READING

LUKE 4:16–32 (NLT)

*When he came to the village of Nazareth, his boyhood home, he went as usual to the synagogue on the Sabbath and stood up to read the Scriptures. The scroll of Isaiah the prophet was handed to him. He unrolled the scroll and found the place where this was written:*

> *"The Spirit of the LORD is upon me,*
> > *for he has anointed me to bring Good News to the poor.*
> *He has sent me to proclaim that captives will be released,*
> > *that the blind will see,*
> *that the oppressed will be set free,*
> > *and that the time of the LORD's favor has come."*

*He rolled up the scroll, handed it back to the attendant, and sat down. All eyes in the synagogue looked at him intently. Then he began to speak to them. "The Scripture you've just heard has been fulfilled this very day!"*

*Everyone spoke well of him and was amazed by the gracious words that came from his lips. "How can this be?" they asked. "Isn't this Joseph's son?"*

*Then he said, "You will undoubtedly quote me this proverb: 'Physician, heal yourself'—meaning, 'Do miracles here in your hometown like those you did in Capernaum.' But I tell you the truth, no prophet is accepted in his own hometown.*

*"Certainly there were many needy widows in Israel in Elijah's time, when the heavens were closed for three and a half years, and a severe famine devastated the land. Yet Elijah was not sent to any of them. He was sent instead to a foreigner—a widow of Zarephath in the land of Sidon. And many in Israel had leprosy in the time of the prophet Elisha, but the only one healed was Naaman, a Syrian."*

*When they heard this, the people in the synagogue were furious. Jumping up, they mobbed him and forced him to the edge of the hill on which the town was built. They intended to push him over the cliff, but he passed right through the crowd and went on his way.*

*Then Jesus went to Capernaum, a town in Galilee, and taught there in the synagogue every Sabbath day. There, too, the people were amazed at his teaching, for he spoke with authority.*

## LIFE LESSONS

Often we see Jesus working in other people's lives but can't see Him working in our own. When this happens, we may become frustrated or even angry. We would do well to pause and remind ourselves that God has a plan. He knows what He's doing even if we can't see it.

When we become frustrated with God, we aren't alone. Those reactions don't surprise Him. By His very nature, nothing surprises Jesus. He knew His path would not be smooth, and He knows that we'll get frustrated, doubt Him, run in the opposite direction, maybe even push Him away like the people in the synagogue did. Nevertheless, we must keep in mind that our paths are firmly in Jesus's hands. He's waiting for us to look to Him, and we can trust Him to guide us.

## WHERE ARE YOU?

*Why did the people in this passage respond to Jesus with respect and then with anger?*

*What do you think it means when it says that Jesus spoke "with authority"?*

*How would you describe your current walk with Jesus?*

_____

_____

_____

_____

_____

## A PRAYER

Jesus, nothing surprises You. You knew exactly what You were getting into by coming to save us, and You did it anyway. Thank You for that. I appreciate Your constant help as I follow Your path for me. Please give me patience and calm when I get angry or frustrated. And help me to celebrate Your work in other people's lives. In Your name, amen.

# DAY 40:
## TURNING IN A NEW DIRECTION

## SCRIPTURE READING

MATTHEW 4:12–17 (CEV)

*When Jesus heard that John had been put in prison, he went to Galilee. But instead of staying in Nazareth, Jesus moved to Capernaum. This town was beside Lake Galilee in the territory of Zebulun and Naphtali. So God's promise came true, just as the prophet Isaiah had said,*

> *"Listen, lands of Zebulun and Naphtali, lands along the road to the sea and across the Jordan. Listen Galilee, land of the Gentiles! Although your people live in darkness, they will see a bright light. Although they live in the shadow of death, a light will shine on them."*

*Then Jesus started preaching, "Turn back to God! The kingdom of heaven will soon be here."*

## LIFE LESSONS

It is Jesus's nature to go where it is dark, to visit places where He has work to do. He wants each of us to live the best life we can—to not feel alone, to not waste our lives in addiction or jealousy, to not feel stuck in destructive ways that only hurt us and our relationships with the people close to us. Jesus's presence brings hope, the ability to climb out of the holes we find ourselves in, a strengthening of community, and so many other things. But transformation doesn't come from nowhere.

Repentance means turning from something to someone. It is a recalibration of our lives and our priorities. It requires turning from our own self-interests. Repentance is essential because it "resets" our relationship with God. This is not a verbal reset. It means actively committing to change, actively turning to Jesus, and committing to following Him and what He says.

Perhaps you're feeling like you've wandered too far. Don't worry. Jesus can find you in the dark.

## WHERE ARE YOU?

*Why does the Bible often refer to Jesus as "the light"?*

_____

_____

_____

_____

*When have you noticed your own life drifting away from God?*

_____

_____

_____

_____

*What do you think Jesus meant when He said, "The kingdom of heaven will soon be here"?*

_____

_____

_____

_____

## A PRAYER

Jesus, thank You for always meeting me where I am. Help me to be quick to turn from my own selfish interests and back to You. Prepare me daily for life with You, now and forever. In Your name, amen.

# DAY 41:
## TRY AND TRY AGAIN

## SCRIPTURE READING

LUKE 5:1–11 (MSG)

*Once when he was standing on the shore of Lake Gennesaret, the crowd was pushing in on him to better hear the Word of God. He noticed two boats tied up. The fishermen had just left them and were out scrubbing their nets. He climbed into the boat that was Simon's and asked him to put out a little from the shore. Sitting there, using the boat for a pulpit, he taught the crowd.*

*When he finished teaching, he said to Simon, "Push out into deep water and let your nets out for a catch."*

*Simon said, "Master, we've been fishing hard all night and haven't caught even a minnow. But if you say so, I'll let out the nets." It was no sooner said than done—a huge haul of fish, straining the nets past capacity. They waved to their partners in the other boat to come help them. They filled both boats, nearly swamping them with the catch.*

*Simon Peter, when he saw it, fell to his knees before Jesus. "Master, leave. I'm a sinner and can't handle this holiness. Leave me to myself." When they pulled in that catch of fish, awe overwhelmed Simon and everyone with him. It was the same with James and John, Zebedee's sons, coworkers with Simon.*

*Jesus said to Simon, "There is nothing to fear. From now on you'll be fishing for men and women." They pulled their boats up on the beach, left them, nets and all, and followed him.*

SEE ALSO: MATTHEW 4:18–22; MARK 1:16–20

## LIFE LESSONS

You don't need to be a fisherman to imagine how it feels to spend a whole night fishing with not even a bite to show for it. You'd be tired. You'd be discouraged. You'd be frustrated. You'd be ready to give up. Someone coming along and offering you unsolicited advice would be the last thing you'd want. Would you have followed Jesus's advice, or would you have ignored it and called it a night?

Jesus's ways are unexpected. He might call you to do something that seems silly or useless—like trying something you've already tried a hundred times before. Don't despair. Keep going and keep your mind open. *Something* is coming. Perhaps the hundred-and-first try is when everything will click into place and really get going. Can you imagine what it will feel like when it does?

Get comfortable saying yes to Jesus. He knows what He's doing. When He asks you to wait, it's often because He has something greater in store than what you were hoping for. Apparent delays that result in abundant blessings can revitalize your faith and the faith of those around you.

## WHERE ARE YOU?

*What was Peter feeling when he fell to his knees?*

_____

_____

_____

_____

_____

*The people around Jesus perceived themselves as His friends. How did Jesus transition them into "disciples"?*

_____

_____

_____

_____

_____

*What keeps you from pursuing the bigger purpose of following Jesus?*

_____

_____

_____

_____

# A PRAYER

Lord Jesus, help me to have faith when it looks like my efforts aren't doing anything. Give me the strength to say yes to You more often, even when I don't feel like it. Thank You for always being there and letting me come back to You over and over again. In Your name, amen.

# DAY 42:
## A REGULAR DAY

## SCRIPTURE READING

MARK 1:21–28 (MSG)

*Then they entered Capernaum. When the Sabbath arrived, Jesus lost no time in getting to the meeting place. He spent the day there teaching. They were surprised at his teaching—so forthright, so confident—not quibbling and quoting like the religion scholars.*

*Suddenly, while still in the meeting place, he was interrupted by a man who was deeply disturbed and yelling out, "What business do you have here with us, Jesus? Nazarene! I know what you're up to! You're the Holy One of God, and you've come to destroy us!"*

*Jesus shut him up: "Quiet! Get out of him!" The afflicting spirit threw the man into spasms, protesting loudly—and got out.*

*Everyone there was spellbound, buzzing with curiosity. "What's going on here? A new teaching that does what it says? He shuts up defiling, demonic spirits and tells them to get lost!" News of this traveled fast and was soon all over Galilee.*

SEE ALSO: LUKE 4:33–37

## LIFE LESSONS

Jesus didn't perform His extraordinary miracles on a grand stage. No spotlight or awards for Him. No, Jesus taught in the synagogue, in the place of worship. On this day, a demon-possessed man, who was probably not new to the synagogue, interrupted Him. Jesus didn't flinch. To Him, interruptions were just that—interruptions. Jesus simply spoke with authority and sent the demon out of the man. No fanfare, no news conference, just a regular day for Jesus—but everyone who saw His actions left in amazement.

Prior to this miracle, the people present in the synagogue had already been moved by Jesus's teaching because He taught as someone with absolute authority. He didn't just recite the laws—He taught as God's Son. Then, when He cast the demon out of the man, Jesus gave onlookers no doubt that not only did He teach with authority, but He was also in control.

We can trust in the fact that, even when we are taken by surprise, Jesus is always in control, and He is *always* ready to act on our behalf.

# WHERE ARE YOU?

*How was Jesus different from the other teachers of the law?*

_____

_____

_____

_____

_____

*What are some markers of someone who teaches "with authority," as Jesus did?*

_____

_____

_____

_____

_____

*Aside from talking about His casting out evil spirits, what do you suppose the people felt and talked about after they saw Jesus?*

_____

_____

_____

_____

_____

# A PRAYER

Lord Jesus, may I never lose my sense of awe at who You are. Remind me daily that everything is within Your control. You do not flinch, You know what is to come, and I can rest in that peace. In Your name, amen.

 DAY 43:
## THE CURE WE NEED

## SCRIPTURE READING

MATTHEW 8:14–15 (CEV)

*Jesus went to the home of Peter, where he found that Peter's mother-in-law was sick in bed with fever. He took her by the hand, and the fever left her. Then she got up and served Jesus a meal.*

SEE ALSO: MARK 1:29–31; LUKE 4:38–39

## LIFE LESSONS

Our world is damaged and sick, and Jesus knows that we will face difficulties in all parts of our lives. He promises to walk with us every step of the way. Not only that, but our God is a healer. He heals physical, emotional, relational, and spiritual wounds. Throughout His earthly ministry, Jesus healed the sick, and, today, Jesus has the cure for your broken life.

Walking with Jesus does not mean that we won't have difficulties—we will still face heartbreak, illnesses, loss of loved ones, financial problems, and all the other painful realities of human existence. The difference lies in the fact that we no longer walk alone. Instead, we walk in the company of the One who can dry our tears with the promise that this life is not the end.

## WHERE ARE YOU?

*Do you think Peter brought Jesus to his house with the expectation that Jesus would heal his mother-in-law?*

*Why do you think Peter's mother-in-law immediately got up and started taking care of Jesus and His disciples upon being healed?*

_____

_____

_____

_____

*Who do you know who is need of Jesus's healing?*

_____

_____

_____

_____

## A PRAYER

Father, I am so grateful to worship a God who loves me and walks with me, who has the power to heal my broken places. I know that, whatever I am going through, You will be there with me to dry my tears. In Jesus's name, amen.

# DAY 44:
## "ALL" AS IN "EVERY SINGLE ONE"

## SCRIPTURE READING

MATTHEW 8:16–17 (NIV)

*When evening came, many who were demon-possessed were brought to him, and he drove out the spirits with a word and healed all the sick. This was to fulfill what was spoken through the prophet Isaiah:*

> *"He took up our infirmities*
> *and bore our diseases."*

SEE ALSO: MARK 1:32–34; LUKE 4:40–41

## LIFE LESSONS

Word that a healer was present spread fast. It didn't take long for a crowd of people in need to form around Jesus. And Jesus didn't comb through the crowd, picking some and leaving others. There was no "This one seems easier but that one looks too far gone." No, Matthew tells us that Jesus *"healed all the sick."*

God has the power to heal no matter how bad the affliction. One word from His mouth can take away our pain and replace it with peace. He can remove our heartache and restore our hope.

If you were sick and heard that a man in another city could heal you with one word, you'd probably be purchasing a plane ticket within seconds. So, why aren't we immediately running to God with our spiritual afflictions and other needs? It's time to run to God today.

# WHERE ARE YOU?

*Why is it important that Jesus fulfilled prophecy?*

_____
_____
_____
_____
_____

*Have you ever considered keeping a record of your daily prayers and praises?*

_____
_____
_____
_____
_____

*How can a prayer journal help you see the work of God in your life?*

_____
_____
_____
_____
_____

# A PRAYER

Dear Jesus, I praise You that You came for all of us, that You are willing and able to heal both our spirits and our physical bodies. I pray that when I need healing and hope, I would run immediately to You. In Your name, amen.

# DAY 45:
## RECONNECT AND RESET

## SCRIPTURE READING

MARK 1:35–39 (NLT)

*Before daybreak the next morning, Jesus got up and went out to an isolated place to pray. Later Simon and the others went out to find him. When they found him, they said, "Everyone is looking for you."*

*But Jesus replied, "We must go on to other towns as well, and I will preach to them, too. That is why I came." So he traveled throughout the region of Galilee, preaching in the synagogues and casting out demons.*

SEE ALSO: MATTHEW 4:23; LUKE 4:42–44

## LIFE LESSONS

Every day, we have the opportunity to take a moment and reset, to make sure we're on course and doing what we're supposed to be doing. Pausing to reconnect with God can get us back on track and help us reprioritize how we spend our time. Prayer can be a great opportunity to reflect on our lives, be reminded of our goals, and let God speak to us and guide us.

Even Jesus needed to spend time with His Father on a daily basis. He needed a quiet place where He could be alone. Jesus came out of His prayer time with a renewed purpose and a clear plan. He knew He needed to move on, to go to other towns to spread His message. It was during Jesus's early morning prayer times that His Father reminded Him of His purpose.

If Jesus needed an isolated place to pray, how much more do we need a place and a time to be alone with God? The hustle and bustle of the world hinders our ability to "be still and know." (See Psalm 46:10 NIV, NLT.) We need some alone time with God so that He can remind us of the purpose for which He has called us.

# WHERE ARE YOU?

*Why would Jesus get up before daybreak?*

_____

_____

_____

_____

_____

*When He knew people were seeking Him, why did Jesus say it was time to move on?*

_____

_____

_____

_____

_____

*How would you describe your prayer life? What can you learn from Jesus's example?*

_____

_____

_____

_____

_____

# A PRAYER

Jesus, help me put aside time every day for You. I know my life is better with You in it. Help me to seek You each day and renew my passion for Your purpose. In Your name, amen.

# DAY 46:
## UP CLOSE AND PERSONAL

## SCRIPTURE READING

LUKE 5:12–16 (NLT)

*In one of the villages, Jesus met a man with an advanced case of leprosy. When the man saw Jesus, he bowed with his face to the ground, begging to be healed. "Lord," he said, "if you are willing, you can heal me and make me clean."*

*Jesus reached out and touched him. "I am willing," he said. "Be healed!" And instantly the leprosy disappeared. Then Jesus instructed him not to tell anyone what had happened. He said, "Go to the priest and let him examine you. Take along the offering required in the law of Moses for those who have been healed of leprosy. This will be a public testimony that you have been cleansed."*

*But despite Jesus's instructions, the report of his power spread even faster, and vast crowds came to hear him preach and to be healed of their diseases. But Jesus often withdrew to the wilderness for prayer.*

SEE ALSO: MATTHEW 8:1–4; MARK 1:40–45

## LIFE LESSONS

Leprosy is a terrible, highly contagious disease. An advanced case of leprosy, such as the man in this passage suffered, would have involved rotten flesh, an incredible stench, and a huge stigma against the victim. When the man stricken with leprosy approached Jesus, he probably kept a respectable distance. But Jesus closed that distance. He reached out and *touched* the man! He didn't linger twenty feet away and shout or wave a hand. He made a point to go to him.

We have a God who touches lepers. Our God is a personal God who reaches down and meets us at our point of need. Jesus is always willing, waiting, and wanting to change our lives.

# WHERE ARE YOU?

*Why was it important that Jesus touched the man in the story?*

_____

_____

_____

_____

_____

*In what way would the touch of Jesus be meaningful to you today?*

_____

_____

_____

_____

_____

*How can you reach those who have been marginalized?*

_____

_____

_____

_____

_____

## A PRAYER

Jesus, You are the Great Healer. You make blind men see and lame men walk. You have the power to cleanse our souls and change our lives. Your willing love and grace work in my life every day. Thank You for meeting me where I am, both physically and spiritually, every time. Amen.

# DAY 47:
## POWER IN SELFLESSNESS

## SCRIPTURE READING

MARK 2:1–12 (MSG)

*After a few days, Jesus returned to Capernaum, and word got around that he was back home. A crowd gathered, jamming the entrance so no one could get in or out. He was teaching the Word. They brought a paraplegic to him, carried by four men. When they weren't able to get in because of the crowd, they removed part of the roof and lowered the paraplegic on his stretcher. Impressed by their bold belief, Jesus said to the paraplegic, "Son, I forgive your sins."*

*Some religion scholars sitting there started whispering among themselves, "He can't talk that way! That's blasphemy! God and only God can forgive sins."*

*Jesus knew right away what they were thinking, and said, "Why are you so skeptical? Which is simpler: to say to the paraplegic, 'I forgive your sins,' or say, 'Get up, take your stretcher, and start walking'? Well, just so it's clear that I'm the Son of Man and authorized to do either, or both..." (he looked now at the paraplegic), "Get up. Pick up your stretcher and go home." And the man did it—got up, grabbed his stretcher, and walked out, with everyone there watching him. They rubbed their eyes, stunned—and then praised God, saying, "We've never seen anything like this!"*

SEE ALSO: MATTHEW 9:1–8; LUKE 5:17–26

## LIFE LESSONS

Just imagine: a packed house, a healer in their midst—yet no one would let a paralyzed man through. The crowd must have known these men were trying to gain entry to bring their friend to the healer's feet, but they didn't bother to make room. That didn't stop the man's friends, though. They went above and beyond, climbing onto the roof and breaking through it. That's dedication!

This story puts the crowd's self-centeredness in sharp contrast with the four men's commitment to see their friend healed. Human nature is selfish, and we can experience these extremes even among believers. It's our nature to focus on ourselves first, often at the expense of others. But look at what the people in the room were able to see when these four friends acted selflessly. The men had so much faith and hope that they were willing to dig through a roof. Jesus responded to their faith, and His power was shown to everyone present.

Following Jesus means becoming more like Him—learning how to love like He did, helping those in need. By caring about others and offering our time and efforts, we selflessly call attention to the power of God, allowing others to see Him working in their lives.

## WHERE ARE YOU?

*Why were the teachers of religious law questioning Jesus?*

*What do you suppose were the reactions of the various people in the house?*

*When has someone gone to great lengths to help you during a difficult time?*

# A PRAYER

Dear Jesus, help me to be a good friend to everyone in my walk with You. Give me the voice to speak out when I see injustice and the courage to value all people. In Your gracious name, amen.

**DAY 48:**
A SENSE OF SOMETHING BETTER

## SCRIPTURE READINGS

MATTHEW 9:9 (NIV)

*As Jesus went on from there, he saw a man named Matthew sitting at the tax collector's booth. "Follow me," he told him, and Matthew got up and followed him.*

MARK 2:13–14 (NIV)

*Once again Jesus went out beside the lake. A large crowd came to him, and he began to teach them. As he walked along, he saw Levi [Matthew] son of Alphaeus sitting at the tax collector's booth. "Follow me," Jesus told him, and Levi got up and followed him.*

SEE ALSO: LUKE 5:27–28

## LIFE LESSONS

In today's world, we often research, talk to friends, look at reviews, and research some more before we make a small decision, like purchasing a couch, much less a large one, like dropping everything and leaving our entire livelihood and community behind. That wasn't the case for some of Jesus's disciples.

Matthew (also called Levi) didn't even think twice. All Jesus had to do was ask, and Matthew just got up and left everything to follow Him—not even knowing exactly what he was getting himself into. He must have sensed that something better was awaiting him.

Something far better is awaiting you as well when you follow Jesus and His teachings. Eventually, it will feel like you've left parts of your old life entirely behind for something greater. It can be terrifying to leave behind what you know, but think of what might be waiting for you on the other side!

# WHERE ARE YOU?

*Why would Matthew leave everything he had to follow Jesus?*

_____

_____

_____

_____

_____

*Has anything ever prompted you to take a step into the unknown?*

_____

_____

_____

_____

_____

*What did Jesus do to cause people to want to be with Him?*

_____

_____

_____

_____

_____

# A PRAYER

Lord Jesus, thank You for inviting me to walk with You. Help me to let go of my old life so I can move forward with nothing holding me back. I know You have incredible things planned for me, and I'm honored to follow You. In Your name, amen.

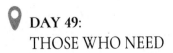 DAY 49:
THOSE WHO NEED

## SCRIPTURE READING

LUKE 5:29–32 (NLT)

*Later, Levi held a banquet in his home with Jesus as the guest of honor. Many of Levi's fellow tax collectors and other guests also ate with them. But the Pharisees and their teachers of religious law complained bitterly to Jesus's disciples, "Why do you eat and drink with such scum?"*

*Jesus answered them, "Healthy people don't need a doctor—sick people do. I have come to call not those who think they are righteous, but those who know they are sinners and need to repent."*

SEE ALSO: MATTHEW 9:10–13; MARK 2:15–17

## LIFE LESSONS

Matthew was a tax collector, and there was not a more hated profession in Jesus's day. (Think of someone from the IRS showing up at your door.) Judgment poured in as Jesus showed up at Matthew's house to dine. People were angry that Jesus would choose the company of this kind of person over theirs.

Jesus asked Matthew to be a disciple and chose to eat with Matthew and his friends because they were the very people who *needed* Him. Jesus was not afraid of what people might think. He had already publicly invited Matthew to be His disciple. He saw something in Matthew, and He wanted other people to see it too.

Jesus wants to be with those who *need* His message. He is willing to go where the sinners are because He sees something in all of us. He is not afraid to sit at the table with those whom most people refuse to accept.

## WHERE ARE YOU?

*How did the Pharisees view outsiders, and what must that have led to?*

_____

_____

_____

_____

_____

*Have you ever been with a group of people who seemed unwelcoming to outsiders?*

_____

_____

_____

_____

_____

*What is Jesus saying to us in this passage?*

_____

_____

_____

_____

_____

## A PRAYER

Jesus, I thank You for eating with the broken, the marginalized, and the outcasts. I praise You for being a personal God who meets us in our time of need. Thank You for making room for me too. In Your name, amen.

## DAY 50:
## ALL ABOUT RELATIONSHIPS

### SCRIPTURE READING

LUKE 5:33–39 (NIV)

*They said to him, "John's disciples often fast and pray, and so do the disciples of the Pharisees, but yours go on eating and drinking."*

*Jesus answered, "Can you make the friends of the bridegroom fast while he is with them? But the time will come when the bridegroom will be taken from them; in those days they will fast."*

*He told them this parable: "No one tears a piece out of a new garment to patch an old one. Otherwise, they will have torn the new garment, and the patch from the new will not match the old. And no one pours new wine into old wineskins. Otherwise, the new wine will burst the skins; the wine will run out and the wineskins will be ruined. No, new wine must be poured into new wineskins. And no one after drinking old wine wants the new, for they say, 'The old is better.'"*

SEE ALSO: MATTHEW 9:14–17; MARK 2:18–22

### LIFE LESSONS

Our culture often sees religion as something boring and restrictive. Sadly, there are reasons for that perception. The word *religion* is associated with depriving yourself, excessive rules, exclusion, and gross intolerance. Even in Jesus's day, people equated proper religious observance with exclusivity and limited freedom. It came down to who could follow all the rules.

Jesus, on the other hand, is all about relationships. And He compared a relationship with Him to a wedding celebration, an event where people enjoy themselves and celebrate with the bride and groom. That doesn't sound like deprivation to me!

Being in Jesus's presence should bring joy, not boredom. Freedom, not restraint. Following Him is about the relationship you have with Him and your relationships with the people around you. It should improve your life and open it up, expand it, not put you in a smaller box and weigh you down.

Jesus's striking analogies of garments and wineskins bring this truth to life. Those two illustrations paint a picture of the stark contrast between a boring religion and a vibrant relationship with Jesus. Our lives should be bigger, not smaller.

They should expand so much that we don't fit into our old lives. Our relationship with Jesus should be a blessing, not a burden. We should be excited about it. If that's not happening, it's time to reset and spend more time with Him.

## WHERE ARE YOU?

*When you were growing up, did you see church as boring and stuffy or full of life?*

_____

_____

_____

_____

*What is the point of the analogies Jesus made of garments and wineskins?*

_____

_____

_____

_____

*Why did Jesus want the Pharisees to experience relationship over ritual?*

_____

_____

_____

_____

## A PRAYER

Jesus, thank You for the joy of a personal relationship with You. Thank You for expanding my life and opening it up so I can see things in new ways. I appreciate Your unending love for me. Help me to regularly celebrate what it means to have Your hope and love in my life. In Your name, amen.

# DAY 51:
## ALMOST TOO SIMPLE

## SCRIPTURE READING

JOHN 5:1–9a (NIV)

*Some time later, Jesus went up to Jerusalem for one of the Jewish festivals. Now there is in Jerusalem near the Sheep Gate a pool, which in Aramaic is called Bethesda and which is surrounded by five covered colonnades. Here a great number of disabled people used to lie—the blind, the lame, the paralyzed. One who was there had been an invalid for thirty-eight years. When Jesus saw him lying there and learned that he had been in this condition for a long time, he asked him, "Do you want to get well?"*

*"Sir," the invalid replied, "I have no one to help me into the pool when the water is stirred. While I am trying to get in, someone else goes down ahead of me."*

*Then Jesus said to him, "Get up! Pick up your mat and walk." At once the man was cured; he picked up his mat and walked.*

## LIFE LESSONS

The Greeks thought that the natural springs at the pool of Bethesda had miraculous healing powers. When the underground springs stirred the pool, the sick would rush to enter it, hoping to find healing.

The paralyzed man in this passage had miserable health and a misplaced hope. Over the course of thirty-eight years, he'd probably lain there hoping against hope that the next time he entered the pool, he would be healed. He'd probably made it in a few times and still wasn't well. After so long, his muscles had probably withered away. So when Jesus asked him such a basic question with such an obvious answer, "Would you like to get well?" the man couldn't even answer directly. He'd lost hope of being truly helped.

Jesus asked that question so the paralyzed man would know that what was about to happen was all Him—not mineral springs, myths, or traditions. Jesus didn't need any of that fluff. He simply told the man, "Stand up, pick up your mat, and walk!" And he did! The man put his hope in Jesus and was healed.

It seems almost too simple. Jesus told the man to walk, and he walked. There were no complicated directions to follow, no rituals to perform. How often do we, too, fail to grasp the simplicity of walking with Jesus?

## WHERE ARE YOU?

*Jesus's question to the man seemed obvious. What do you think the man was pondering in this conversation?*

_____

_____

_____

_____

_____

*Why would he trust Jesus so quickly and without question?*

_____

_____

_____

_____

_____

*Are there any areas in which you are struggling to trust Jesus? If so, pray about them now, asking Him to help you release your cares to Him.*

_____

_____

_____

_____

_____

## A PRAYER

Father, thank You for Your miracle-working power. Thank You for stepping into my life and changing everything—for picking me up and putting me back on my feet again! Help me to walk daily with You. In Jesus's name, amen.

# DAY 52:
## LOOK FOR THE POSITIVE

## SCRIPTURE READING

JOHN 5:9b–15 (NIV)

*The day on which this took place was a Sabbath, and so the Jewish leaders said to the man who had been healed, "It is the Sabbath; the law forbids you to carry your mat."*

*But he replied, "The man who made me well said to me, 'Pick up your mat and walk.'"*

*So they asked him, "Who is this fellow who told you to pick it up and walk?"*

*The man who was healed had no idea who it was, for Jesus had slipped away into the crowd that was there.*

*Later Jesus found him at the temple and said to him, "See, you are well again. Stop sinning or something worse may happen to you." The man went away and told the Jewish leaders that it was Jesus who had made him well.*

## LIFE LESSONS

The religious crowd should have been ecstatic for this man who was healed. Instead, they were upset because he carried his mat on the Sabbath. Can you imagine being this man? After all these years, you can finally walk. This incredible thing just happened that will alter the course of your life. And all the religious circle cares about is that you are "working" on the Sabbath by carrying your mat!

Petty people love to throw water on the Spirit's fire. Something is terribly wrong with religion when we can't get excited about a dramatic change for the better in someone's life. Such pettiness leads those who do not walk with Jesus to assume that rules and regulations and finger-pointing are the core of Christ's story.

Ultimately, we all find what our hearts seek. The religious leaders found what they were looking for in condemning Jesus's miracle through a Sabbath technicality. And even today, if we are always looking for something wrong, we will usually find it. Instead, look for what's right. Look for what's positive and uplifting.

## WHERE ARE YOU?

*How might this story have ended differently if the man had considered the Sabbath and refused to pick up his mat?*

_____

_____

_____

_____

_____

*Do you think some religious people today "miss the miracles" because they are preoccupied with how things ought to be done?*

_____

_____

_____

_____

_____

*Has skepticism ever prevented you from celebrating a miracle?*

_____

_____

_____

_____

_____

## A PRAYER

Father, help my heart to seek Your love and not fall into the trap of following rules for rules' sake. Help me to find reasons to rejoice in all things that come from You and to celebrate with those whose lives are being touched by You. I pray that I would never throw water on Your Spirit's fire. In Jesus's name, amen.

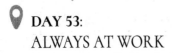

## DAY 53:
## ALWAYS AT WORK

## SCRIPTURE READING

JOHN 5:16–30 (NLT)

*So the Jewish leaders began harassing Jesus for breaking the Sabbath rules. But Jesus replied, "My Father is always working, and so am I." So the Jewish leaders tried all the harder to find a way to kill him. For he not only broke the Sabbath, he called God his Father, thereby making himself equal with God.*

*So Jesus explained, "I tell you the truth, the Son can do nothing by himself. He does only what he sees the Father doing. Whatever the Father does, the Son also does. For the Father loves the Son and shows him everything he is doing. In fact, the Father will show him how to do even greater works than healing this man. Then you will truly be astonished. For just as the Father gives life to those he raises from the dead, so the Son gives life to anyone he wants. In addition, the Father judges no one. Instead, he has given the Son absolute authority to judge, so that everyone will honor the Son, just as they honor the Father. Anyone who does not honor the Son is certainly not honoring the Father who sent him.*

*"I tell you the truth, those who listen to my message and believe in God who sent me have eternal life. They will never be condemned for their sins, but they have already passed from death into life.*

*"And I assure you that the time is coming, indeed it's here now, when the dead will hear my voice—the voice of the Son of God. And those who listen will live. The Father has life in himself, and he has granted that same life-giving power to his Son. And he has given him authority to judge everyone because he is the Son of Man. Don't be so surprised! Indeed, the time is coming when all the dead in their graves will hear the voice of God's Son, and they will rise again. Those who have done good will rise to experience eternal life, and those who have continued in evil will rise to experience judgment. I can do nothing on my own. I judge as God tells me. Therefore, my judgment is just, because I carry out the will of the one who sent me, not my own will."*

## LIFE LESSONS

Again, you would think the religious leaders would have been awestruck to see a man who had lain paralyzed for thirty-eight years stand up and walk.

Instead, they harassed Jesus for healing a paralyzed man on the Sabbath, making sure He knew He had picked the wrong day to heal. They should have been taking in the miracle that had just occurred and applauding Jesus; instead, they were nitpicking *when* Jesus had chosen to do that miracle.

Jesus's response? "My Father is always working, and so am I." *God is always working, so I am always working.*

There are two profound points in this statement. First, Jesus referred to God as His Father, making Him God's equal. Coming from anyone else, this would be considered blasphemous, so it was sure to turn heads His way in anger. Second, He and God are *always* at work. He plans to continue working 24/7, and He's planning even *greater* works. The people in Jesus's day hadn't seen anything yet. Jesus was just getting started.

Jesus never stops working. There is no time when He won't be available or won't be looking out for you. There is never a reason for Him to stop, and you can rest assured that He will be working regardless of the day, time, or circumstances.

## WHERE ARE YOU?

*If Jesus was doing good, why were some leaders harassing Him?*

_____

_____

_____

_____

*In your own words, how would you summarize Jesus's response to them?*

_____

_____

_____

_____

*What does it mean to you that Jesus is always working on your behalf?*

_____

_____

_____

_____

_____

## A PRAYER

Jesus, thank You for Your power to heal, restore, and raise the dead to life. I am continually amazed by You. It encourages me today to know that You and Your Father are always working. In Your name, amen.

# DAY 54:
# DON'T MISS THE FOREST FOR THE TREES

## SCRIPTURE READING

### JOHN 5:31–47 (NLT)

*"If I were to testify on my own behalf, my testimony would not be valid. But someone else is also testifying about me, and I assure you that everything he says about me is true. In fact, you sent investigators to listen to John the Baptist, and his testimony about me was true. Of course, I have no need of human witnesses, but I say these things so you might be saved. John was like a burning and shining lamp, and you were excited for a while about his message. But I have a greater witness than John— my teachings and my miracles. The Father gave me these works to accomplish, and they prove that he sent me. And the Father who sent me has testified about me himself. You have never heard his voice or seen him face to face, and you do not have his message in your hearts, because you do not believe me—the one he sent to you.*

*"You search the Scriptures because you think they give you eternal life. But the Scriptures point to me! Yet you refuse to come to me to receive this life.*

*"Your approval means nothing to me, because I know you don't have God's love within you. For I have come to you in my Father's name, and you have rejected me. Yet if others come in their own name, you gladly welcome them. No wonder you can't believe! For you gladly honor each other, but you don't care about the honor that comes from the one who alone is God.*

*"Yet it isn't I who will accuse you before the Father. Moses will accuse you! Yes, Moses, in whom you put your hopes. If you really believed Moses, you would believe me, because he wrote about me. But since you don't believe what he wrote, how will you believe what I say?"*

## LIFE LESSONS

Jesus highlighted a major error in the way the religious crowd approached their relationship with God—an error that prevented them from seeing Jesus for who He was. They embraced an academic mindset toward God and Scripture and prioritized that over a relationship with Him. The same problem happens to many people today, and it keeps them from having a right relationship with Jesus.

It's easy for Jesus's message to get masked by religious leaders and others who call themselves His followers but don't live out His words. They don't act the way Jesus did, they don't demonstrate His unending love and all-inclusive acceptance, and they don't point toward His grace and sacrifice. But they know their Scripture.

Jesus emphasizes that the point of the Scriptures is to guide people to Him. It's possible *for any of us* to read and study the Word of God and miss Jesus entirely. Churches and individuals alike do this at times. If our emphasis is on the study of God's Word rather than seeking a relationship with Jesus, we reduce the journey to an academic task. If we aren't careful, we may find ourselves seeking knowledge over relationship. We miss the forest for the trees and forget the whole reason the Scriptures are there.

The purpose of studying the Bible is to be pointed to Jesus. Don't stop at mere head knowledge!

## WHERE ARE YOU?

*What criticism or warning does Jesus offer in this passage?*

*Do you know anyone who seems familiar with the stories of Jesus and even knows the Scriptures yet hasn't demonstrated a changed life? If so, why do you think this is the case?*

*How have the life of Jesus and the Word of God changed you?*

_____

_____

_____

_____

_____

## A PRAYER

Lord God, thank You for the priceless gift of Your Word. I want to know You more. Give me wisdom and help me to study Scripture by focusing on a relationship and not a religion. In Jesus's name, amen.

## DAY 55:
## IT'S NOT ABOUT THE LIST

## SCRIPTURE READING

MATTHEW 12:1–8 (NLT)

*At about that time Jesus was walking through some grainfields on the Sabbath. His disciples were hungry, so they began breaking off some heads of grain and eating them. But some Pharisees saw them do it and protested, "Look, your disciples are breaking the law by harvesting grain on the Sabbath."*

*Jesus said to them, "Haven't you read in the Scriptures what David did when he and his companions were hungry? He went into the house of God, and he and his companions broke the law by eating the sacred loaves of bread that only the priests are allowed to eat. And haven't you read in the law of Moses that the priests on duty in the Temple may work on the Sabbath? I tell you, there is one here who is even greater than the Temple! But you would not have condemned my innocent disciples if you knew the meaning of this Scripture: 'I want you to show mercy, not offer sacrifices.' For the Son of Man is Lord, even over the Sabbath!"*

SEE ALSO: MARK 2:23–28; LUKE 6:1–5

## LIFE LESSONS

The religious leaders in Jesus's day were more concerned about making rules and following them than they were about spending time with God on the Lord's Day. To them, the Sabbath was all about sticking to intricate rules, down to the tiniest footnotes—which ended up creating many ways for people to fail but failing to help people build a relationship with God. Relationships are built through spending time together.

The Pharisees didn't understand the Sabbath (Jesus's day) because they didn't know Jesus—which is why they dared to reprimand Him about the way He chose to spend this day.

Remember that the Sabbath is simply a day to rest with God. There's no list to follow. There aren't checkboxes you need to fill to appropriately observe your Sabbath. Lose the list and do what brings you closer to God, whatever that is. Don't let anyone tell you how to go about it properly. Just spend time with Him.

# WHERE ARE YOU?

*How has observing the Sabbath changed over time?*

_____

_____

_____

_____

_____

*In what ways did Jesus's teaching about the Sabbath signify a shift in thinking?*

_____

_____

_____

_____

_____

*What did Jesus mean when He quoted the Old Testament by saying, "I want you to show mercy, not offer sacrifices" (Matthew 12:7 NLT; see Hosea 6:6)?*

_____

_____

_____

_____

_____

# A PRAYER

Jesus, thank You for valuing me, my life, and spending time with me more than You value my living up to specific standards. Thank You for breaking those standards by coming down to earth to be with us. I know that all days are Your days. Help me to spend them in Your presence in a way that resonates with my soul. In Your name, amen.

# DAY 56:
## KEEPING OUR EYES ON OURSELVES

## SCRIPTURE READING

MATTHEW 12:9–14 (NIV)

*Going on from that place, he went into their synagogue, and a man with a shriveled hand was there. Looking for a reason to bring charges against Jesus, they asked him, "Is it lawful to heal on the Sabbath?"*

*He said to them, "If any of you has a sheep and it falls into a pit on the Sabbath, will you not take hold of it and lift it out? How much more valuable is a person than a sheep! Therefore it is lawful to do good on the Sabbath."*

*Then he said to the man, "Stretch out your hand." So he stretched it out and it was completely restored, just as sound as the other. But the Pharisees went out and plotted how they might kill Jesus.*

SEE ALSO: MARK 3:1–6; LUKE 6:6–11

## LIFE LESSONS

The religious leaders in this passage are *eagerly* waiting to find fault with Jesus instead of trying to understand Him and what He's telling them. It is genuinely disheartening to know that they spent more time scrutinizing Jesus than they did listening to Him—true masters at the game of "gotcha!"

Have you ever found yourself starting to play that game? Do you wait for other people to mess up? Do you discuss other people's faults with those around you? If we're not careful, we too can spend our energy pointing out the shortcomings of others, and that's a road that leads directly opposite of where we want to be.

Don't fall into that trap! If you find yourself fixating on someone else and what they're doing, contemplate what you can do to lift them up, without nitpicking or judgment. And even more, keep your eyes on your own relationship with God. If you're too busy worrying about someone else's faith journey, you'll neglect your own.

## WHERE ARE YOU?

*Why do you think the religious leaders continued to find fault with Jesus?*

_____

_____

_____

_____

*How does it make you feel when you see one believer zero in on the shortcomings of another?*

_____

_____

_____

_____

*How can you keep your focus on Christ when others are pointing out your faults?*

_____

_____

_____

_____

## A PRAYER

Jesus, help me to keep my eyes on You and to focus on my walk with You, not anyone else's. I pray to be kind above everything else. Don't let judging others overtake me. Let my actions lift other people up. In Your name, amen.

# DAY 57:
## SPREAD THE HOPE

## SCRIPTURE READING

MARK 3:7–12 (CEV)

*Jesus led his disciples down to the shore of the lake. Large crowds followed him from Galilee, Judea, and Jerusalem. People came from Idumea, as well as other places east of the Jordan River. They also came from the region around the towns of Tyre and Sidon. All of these crowds came because they had heard what Jesus was doing. He even had to tell his disciples to get a boat ready to keep him from being crushed by the crowds.*

*After Jesus had healed many people, the other sick people begged him to let them touch him. And whenever any evil spirits saw Jesus, they would fall to the ground and shout, "You are the Son of God!" But Jesus warned the spirits not to tell who he was.*

SEE ALSO: MATTHEW 4:23–25; 12:15–21

## LIFE LESSONS

It's incredible how quickly and how far the news of Jesus traveled simply by word of mouth. Positive stories of personal experiences mean so much to people, as we can see in today's passage. The accounts of healing and miracles spreading throughout the region brought *multitudes* of people—so many that Jesus had to get off land in order to avoid getting hurt. Imagine an arena of people flocking to see a popular musician today. That's how eager people were to see Jesus. It couldn't have been easy for most of them to travel to see Him, either, but they had family and friends showing up in their hometowns healed, hopeful, and raving about Jesus, so they knew the trip would be worth the effort.

In today's world, bad news often spreads faster than good news, especially as it makes its rounds via the Internet. It can be much harder for stories of hope to go viral. One of the best ways we can spread and confirm the hope of Jesus is by living a life that demonstrates Christ's love. We can personally share what's happened in our lives and in the lives of people we know. Seeing transformed people up close is a game changer.

## WHERE ARE YOU?

*Why do you think Jesus asked for a boat?*

_____

_____

_____

_____

_____

*In your view, why were so many people seeking out Jesus?*

_____

_____

_____

_____

*Why did Jesus command the spirits not to reveal who He was?*

_____

_____

_____

_____

_____

## A PRAYER

Jesus, I am in awe of Your power and might. You have no rival, and You stand above all others. I pray that my life would be an example to other people, showing Your power to heal and bring about change. I pray that the way I live my life would bring hope to others as well. In Your name, amen.

OUR INVITATION

## SCRIPTURE READING

MARK 3:13–19 (NLT)

*Afterward Jesus went up on a mountain and called out the ones he wanted to go with him. And they came to him. Then he appointed twelve of them and called them his apostles. They were to accompany him, and he would send them out to preach, giving them authority to cast out demons. These are the twelve he chose:*

> *Simon (whom he named Peter),*
> *James and John (the sons of Zebedee, but Jesus nicknamed them*
> *"Sons of Thunder"),*
> *Andrew,*
> *Philip,*
> *Bartholomew,*
> *Matthew,*
> *Thomas,*
> *James (son of Alphaeus),*
> *Thaddaeus,*
> *Simon (the zealot),*
> *Judas Iscariot (who later betrayed him).*

SEE ALSO: LUKE 6:12–16

## LIFE LESSONS

In this passage we read of Jesus's invitation to His first disciples. It describes how He called those with whom He wanted to minister. The call He gave to these first disciples is the same call He gives to us today: to follow Him. What does that mean? Let's take a closer look at these verses.

First, we are to enjoy His presence. Mark 3:14 states, "*They were to accompany him*" (NLT). Jesus calls us to follow Him so that we might have fellowship with Him. We are to learn from His life. We are to spend time in His presence.

Second, we are to expand His purpose. Mark 3:14 continues, "*He would send them out to preach*" (NLT). Enjoying Jesus's presence empowers us to be an extension of His life and teaching. It puts us in touch with His greater purpose.

And, finally, we are to experience His power. Mark 3:15 reveals that God sent the disciples out with *His* power, *"giving them authority to cast out demons"* (NLT). They were given authority to be Christ's disciples. God provides us with everything we need to live out the journey He has called us to.

We are called today to show our friends, family members, coworkers—everyone we encounter throughout our day—who Jesus is and how to follow Him. We can direct people to Jesus through our actions. If we live and love like Jesus, we bring people to know Him.

## WHERE ARE YOU?

*Do you think Jesus's selection of the apostles was random, or did God guide Jesus to select the chosen twelve? Why?*

_____

_____

_____

_____

_____

*Why was it important that the apostles were asked to "accompany" Jesus?*

_____

_____

_____

_____

*What do you think the passage means when it says the apostles were given "authority to cast out demons" (Mark 3:15 NLT)?*

_____

_____

_____

_____

_____

## A PRAYER

Jesus, thank You for the privilege of spending time in Your presence. May my focus be on Your purpose for which I was created. Lord, I long to experience Your power through my life. Help me to surrender my will to Yours. In Your name, amen.

 **DAY 59:**
## HEALING IN ALL ITS FORMS

## SCRIPTURE READING

### MATTHEW 4:24–25 (NIV)

*News about him spread all over Syria, and people brought to him all who were ill with various diseases, those suffering severe pain, the demon-possessed, those having seizures, and the paralyzed; and he healed them. Large crowds from Galilee, the Decapolis, Jerusalem, Judea and the region across the Jordan followed him.*

## LIFE LESSONS

Everyone loves to see power on display. We live in a world that worships the miraculous, the sensational. We're drawn to spectacles. We like to be amazed, and the same was true in Jesus's time.

Jesus drew crowds wherever He went, and everyone wanted to touch Him because they had witnessed the healing power that radiated from Him. Miracles don't have to be just physical, though. What if we wanted to get close to Jesus as much for spiritual healing as we did for physical healing? What would happen in our world if we were to seek healing for our broken natures as much as we sought healing for our broken bodies?

We all need to shift our views and remember to celebrate not only the material and physical transformations, but also the emotional and spiritual ones. It's just as incredible when someone overcomes an addiction, heals from the scars of their past, or turns away from a toxic relationship. Those transformations are also life-changing—and eternity-changing—and deserve our amazement and praise.

## WHERE ARE YOU?

*Why do you think it was important that those around Jesus saw Him perform miracles?*

_____

_____

_____

_____

_____

*Have you ever known anyone to reject Jesus because they haven't witnessed a miracle?*

_____

_____

_____

_____

_____

*What would you say to someone who insists on seeing a miracle in order to believe in Jesus?*

_____

_____

_____

_____

_____

## A PRAYER

Jesus, thank You for healing not only our physical bodies but our spirits, hearts, and minds as well. Help me to never lose respect for the authority of Your Word and presence. Help me to love You and see Your Spirit in all things. In Your name, amen.

# DAY 60:
## GOD BLESSES

## SCRIPTURE READING
...................................................................................................

MATTHEW 5:1–12 (NIV)

*Now when Jesus saw the crowds, he went up on a mountainside and sat down. His disciples came to him, and he began to teach them.*

*He said:*

> *"Blessed are the poor in spirit,*
>> *for theirs is the kingdom of heaven.*
> *Blessed are those who mourn,*
>> *for they will be comforted.*
> *Blessed are the meek,*
>> *for they will inherit the earth.*
> *Blessed are those who hunger and thirst for righteousness,*
>> *for they will be filled.*
> *Blessed are the merciful,*
>> *for they will be shown mercy.*
> *Blessed are the pure in heart,*
>> *for they will see God.*
> *Blessed are the peacemakers,*
>> *for they will be called children of God.*
> *Blessed are those who are persecuted because of righteousness,*
>> *for theirs is the kingdom of heaven.*

*"Blessed are you when people insult you, persecute you and falsely say all kinds of evil against you because of me. Rejoice and be glad, because great is your reward in heaven, for in the same way they persecuted the prophets who were before you."*

SEE ALSO: LUKE 6:20–26

## LIFE LESSONS

This passage is the beginning of what's known as the Sermon on the Mount, and these opening verses in particular are known as "The Beatitudes." They express Jesus's core values, identifying the attitudes that should be present in the life of every believer.

In Matthew's account, there are eight statements that begin with the words *"Blessed are...."* God longs to bless us and to lead us to a life of authentic joy and peace, but we have to approach Him with an open heart and the right attitude.

A relationship with Jesus blesses us to think and live differently in terms of what we value for this journey and how our lives impact those around us. When we look to Jesus for what to value in this life and the next, we truly can experience the blessing of His presence and be a blessing to other people. If we want to start living like Jesus, the Beatitudes open us to humble ourselves so God can work in us and through us.

There will be other rewards that await us in heaven, but our lives on earth can be blessed when we live out God's will for our earthly journey.

## WHERE ARE YOU?

*What are the core values Jesus reveals in the Beatitudes?*

_____

_____

_____

_____

_____

*Can you think of a place in Scripture where Jesus exemplifies one of the Beatitudes?*

_____

_____

_____

_____

_____

*Which of the Beatitudes speaks most to you, and why?*

_____

_____

_____

_____

_____

## A PRAYER

Jesus, thank You for the blessings You bring to those who live according to Your Word. I pray that I would have the appropriate attitude and perspective to seek Your blessings over the things of this world. Help me to live differently. In Your name, amen.

# DAY 61:
## LIVING TO THE FULLEST

## SCRIPTURE READINGS

MATTHEW 5:3 (NIV)

*Blessed are the poor in spirit, for theirs is the kingdom of heaven.*

LUKE 6:20 (NIV)

*Looking at his disciples, he said:*

> *"Blessed are you who are poor,*
> *for yours is the kingdom of God."*

## LIFE LESSONS

What does it mean to be poor, according to these verses? There are several biblical words that translate into English as "poor." One word speaks of poverty, while another describes someone who is absolutely destitute, as in having nothing to their name. The word translated as *"poor"* in today's verses means "to cringe, to cower, and to shrink back." It implies being as helpless as a beggar, with no sense of pride, only an instinct for survival.

Jesus is saying that our lives will be blessed when we realize at our core that He is all we need. And that is how we should seek Him: as though our lives depend on it, fully aware we can't do it on our own. We can build up earthly things around us to feel secure—possessions, powerful people, prestigious careers—but we *need* God. We are helpless without Him. Only when we possess what God provides do we have everything we need. When we let go of our pride and admit our need, we are ready to follow Him and live fully.

## WHERE ARE YOU?

*What are some attributes of a good life, according to the world's standards?*

_____

_____

_____

_____

_____

*Is it possible to possess material wealth and still receive the blessings of God? Why or why not?*

_____

_____

_____

_____

_____

*How can we balance our physical needs with our walk with Jesus?*

_____

_____

_____

_____

_____

## A PRAYER

Jesus, please help me to empty myself of everything before You. Never let me forget that it is through You that I have anything and everything. I am helpless without You. Let me live fully aware of my need for You. I love You, Lord. In Your name, amen.

# DAY 62:
## LOVING TO THE FULLEST

## SCRIPTURE READINGS

MATTHEW 5:4 (NIV)

*Blessed are those who mourn, for they will be comforted.*

LUKE 6:21b (NIV)

*Blessed are you who weep now, for you will laugh.*

## LIFE LESSONS

Love, at its deepest level, is a risky step in a broken world, but love also transforms life. We are blessed when we risk loving to the point of great loss, but often we shy away from deep relationships because we fear losing what we love, be it a person or a passion.

The word *"blessed"* here can be defined as an inward contentment despite outward circumstances. Notice that Jesus did not say, "God blesses those who moan." This Scripture is not speaking about those who constantly drink from the cup of self-pity! Jesus is speaking of those who truly mourn, those who have risked loving with their whole heart—those who put everything out there.

We live in a world that has tried everything to numb the pain of broken relationships and loss. Jesus tells us that when we authentically love like He does, we live to our fullest. And even in the loss of whom and what we love most, we can bring our pain to Him. God provides comfort even in the most difficult circumstances. He never promised that this life would be easy, but He did promise He would never leave us or forsake us. When you feel frustrated or afraid, when you are faced with loss, remember that peace is not the absence of conflict; rather, it is the presence of Jesus through all situations of life.

## WHERE ARE YOU?

*What is the greatest loss you have mourned in your life?*

_____

_____

_____

_____

_____

*Have you ever found yourself feeling blessed in the midst of a loss? How so?*

_____

_____

_____

_____

_____

*What spiritual resources help you to cope with loss?*

_____

_____

_____

_____

_____

## A PRAYER

Jesus, thank You for being a God of comfort and strength. Help me to open myself up to love in all areas of my life. Remind me to seek You when I mourn. Thank You for being present when I'm struggling. Thank You for the comfort You bring. In Your name, amen.

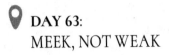

**DAY 63:**
MEEK, NOT WEAK

## SCRIPTURE READING

MATTHEW 5:5 (NIV)

*Blessed are the meek, for they will inherit the earth.*

## LIFE LESSONS

Many different Bible versions translate the first phrase of this verse as *"Blessed are the meek."* Yet the idea that those who are meek are blessed does not reflect our popular culture's way of thinking. Our society tends to see meekness as a sign of weakness. A meek person is often thought of as mousy and timid.

However, the New Testament word is *praus,* which means *exercising God's strength under control.* An illustration of this would be bridling a wild horse. The wild horse is still strong—the bridle doesn't change that fact—but the bridle allows the horse to use that strength under another's control. When we continually approach Jesus with humility, knowing that His power is greater than ours and recognizing our own need, that is when He can use us for His purpose in our lives—and that is when we can do greater things than we could ever do without Him.

## WHERE ARE YOU?

*How is meekness different from weakness?*

_____

_____

_____

_____

_____

*How can you maintain a meek or humble posture in a culture that promotes assertion and aggression?*

_____

_____

_____

_____

_____

*How does the analogy of bridling a wild horse parallel someone who chooses to be humble in the sight of God?*

_____

_____

_____

_____

_____

_____

## A PRAYER

Jesus, thank You for being the perfect example of power under control, humbling Yourself to be obedient to Your Father's will and giving Your life so we could live. In Your name, amen.

# DAY 64:
## COUNTERCULTURAL CRAVINGS

## SCRIPTURE READINGS

MATTHEW 5:6 (NIV)

*Blessed are those who hunger and thirst for righteousness, for they will be filled.*

LUKE 6:21a (NIV)

*Blessed are you who hunger now, for you will be satisfied.*

## LIFE LESSONS

Do you remember the last time you felt like you couldn't go one step farther unless you got something to eat? What about the last time you were *really* thirsty? All you could think about was where you would get your next meal or that next sip of water.

Jesus wants us to crave His presence in our lives, to long for Him, to approach our walk with Him like a starving person would go after food. Realistically, the world hungers for things like possessions, success, and popularity. We live in a culture that hungers for more of *this world*. When a person hungers and thirsts after righteousness, they are insatiable in their need to be close to Christ and to experience everything that walking with Him entails.

When we walk with Jesus, we walk counter-culturally to this world. Possessions don't matter as much, fitting in doesn't matter as much, being at the top doesn't matter as much. What does start to matter are the things God cares about, like being kind to others, showing up for our friends, and giving to the needy with our time and resources. When we walk with Jesus in a world seeking satisfaction through success, we realize true satisfaction is found only in a relationship with Him. By loving Jesus and loving like Him, we will have the deepest needs of our hearts met by God.

# WHERE ARE YOU?

*Describe a time when you were absolutely famished with hunger.*

_____

_____

_____

_____

*Do you think that someone who is hungry for righteousness could have the same degree of yearning to be filled as someone who hasn't eaten in days?*

_____

_____

_____

_____

*When we hunger for righteousness, what can we do to fill our need?*

_____

_____

_____

_____

# A PRAYER

Jesus, I pray that a desire for possessions and success would never take over my heart. Help me to remember that true contentment comes through You. I want to care about the things You care about. I want my mind to focus on higher things. Give me a hunger for You, Your presence, Your words. In Your name, amen.

# DAY 65:
## EVERYDAY MERCY

## SCRIPTURE READING

MATTHEW 5:7 (NIV)

*Blessed are the merciful, for they will be shown mercy.*

## LIFE LESSONS

There is a saying that forgiven people forgive people. Mercy is the act of forgiving. Those who have been given mercy tend to show mercy to others. It's reciprocal. And that comes from our own relationship with God.

Mercy and grace are the essence of God's love for us. Mercy is the compassion of God in action. God has forgiven us, and we should show others that same compassion. When we love like Jesus, we cannot help but offer the same grace He has already shown us.

To be unmerciful is to be unlike Jesus at the most basic level. We commit seemingly insignificant non-merciful acts every day: holding a grudge, excluding others, speaking unkind words, acting selfishly. Sometimes we also withhold mercy in more significant ways. Regardless, true mercy responds with grace, forgives fully, and moves forward.

Think of a world in which people act out of grace and mercy in their everyday interactions. How different that would be from what we experience now! What a beautiful world that would be. *That* is the vision of God's kingdom.

## WHERE ARE YOU?

*Who will be shown mercy, according to today's verse?*

_____

_____

_____

_____

_____

*Why is it so hard to forgive others when they hurt us?*

_____

_____

_____

_____

_____

*It is often said that we should "forgive and forget." What keeps you from being able to forget?*

_____

_____

_____

_____

_____

## A PRAYER

Lord Jesus, please help me to forgive others and to always show mercy out of my gratitude for all the mercy You have shown to me. Thank You for being rich in mercy and that Your mercies are new every morning. In Your name, amen.

# DAY 66:
## AN UNDIVIDED HEART

## SCRIPTURE READING

MATTHEW 5:8 (NIV)

*Blessed are the pure in heart, for they will see God.*

## LIFE LESSONS

From the Greek word for "pure" in this passage, *katharos*, we get our English word *catharsis*, referring to purification or renewal through purging. The Greek word implies something that is absolutely pure or clean. Nothing has been added to it; nothing else is soiling its purity. In other words, "Blessed are those who don't have divided or mixed hearts."

When we think about a pure heart, we may think about someone who always seems to do the right things. They must be pure, right? But that's not exactly what Jesus is talking about; that's focusing solely on the external. God looks at our hearts, at the internal, at our deepest desires. He wants our hearts' desire to be Him over everything else—not split between Him and something else. Similar to the idea of single-mindedness, He wants us to have singleness of heart.

God wants to be our heart's ultimate motivation and ultimate destination. A heart in line with Jesus leads to a life in line with Jesus. Someone who wants nothing more than to be with and love God will have their heart transformed from the inside out. Pure actions will reflect their pure heart.

## WHERE ARE YOU?

*In your own words, who will see God?*

_____
_____
_____
_____
_____

*Do you know anyone who indicates by their life that they have a pure heart? What are some of those indications?*

_____
_____
_____
_____
_____

*What are some ways of purifying the heart?*

_____
_____
_____
_____
_____

## A PRAYER

God, help me to reflect on my own heart's desires. Reveal to me what might be holding me back from having a pure heart. Show me if my heart is divided between a love for you and a love for the things of this world. Help me to refocus on You so my actions and decisions will be pure ones, coming from a heart devoted to You. In Jesus's name, amen.

## DAY 67:
## ACTIVE PEACE

## SCRIPTURE READING
· · · · · · · · · · · · · · · · · · · · · · · · · · · · · · · · · · · · · · · · · · · · · · · · · · · · · · · · · · · · · · · · · · · · · ·

MATTHEW 5:9 (NIV)

*Blessed are the peacemakers, for they will be called children of God.*

## LIFE LESSONS
· · · · · · · · · · · · · · · · · · · · · · · · · · · · · · · · · · · · · · · · · · · · · · · · · · · · · · · · · · · · · · · · · · · · · ·

Peace is not always passive. Working for peace does not always mean just letting things go or sitting silently in your room enjoying the quiet. It comes from effort and action, from walking toward or into conflict with the hope of reconciliation. It can mean taking on hard conversations or assisting others with healing.

Everyone, including Christians, seems to experience more conflict than peace: conflict with others, with ourselves, and with God. In our friend groups, families, churches, and other relationships, conflict is constantly disrupting peace. Most issues don't resolve fully on their own. People need to be asked to speak more politely, to back down a bit, to consider another side, to apologize, to learn, and so on. Plans need to be created for resolution; agreements must be suggested for the arranged withdrawal of two parties. At times we may be called to greater action, like marching with one side to remind others of what could create true peace.

Peace won't always follow, despite our efforts. It may even seem pointless at times to try to seek peace, but we're called to seek it anyway, meaning we're called to love like Jesus and promote the truth. That may not sound like many people's idea of peace. But peace is not avoidance; it is bringing truth and honesty to the world, even in the darkness and the discord. One of Jesus's first names in Scripture is the Prince of Peace. If we are seeking to love like Jesus, peacemaking is an act we must take on.

## WHERE ARE YOU?

*Why do you think Jesus calls peacemakers "children of God"?*

_____

_____

_____

_____

_____

*When have you been called upon to be a peacemaker?*

_____

_____

_____

_____

_____

*Peace is such a prominent theme among Christian believers, yet there is still so much conflict in the world. Why do you think that is the case?*

_____

_____

_____

_____

_____

## A PRAYER

Jesus, You are the Prince of Peace. Help me to become a peacemaker. Help me to promote truth and be brave enough to step into conflict to speak peace and truth to all situations. I know I can only do this through You. In Your name, amen.

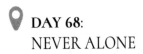

# DAY 68:
# NEVER ALONE

## SCRIPTURE READINGS

MATTHEW 5:10–12 (NIV)

*Blessed are those who are persecuted because of righteousness, for theirs is the kingdom of heaven.*

*Blessed are you when people insult you, persecute you and falsely say all kinds of evil against you because of me. Rejoice and be glad, because great is your reward in heaven, for in the same way they persecuted the prophets who were before you.*

LUKE 6:22–23 (NIV)

*Blessed are you when people hate you, when they exclude you and insult you and reject your name as evil, because of the Son of Man.*

*Rejoice in that day and leap for joy, because great is your reward in heaven. For that is how their ancestors treated the prophets.*

## LIFE LESSONS

Jesus closed out the Beatitudes with a perspective on persecution that contradicts the popular health-wealth gospel of our day. Unfortunately, nowhere does Scripture teach that if you give your life to Jesus, all your problems will disappear. On the contrary, Jesus Himself was persecuted because of how He lived His life: teaching what He did, performing miracles on the Sabbath, and hanging out with people on the lower rungs of society. While few of us will be persecuted in the sense of being imprisoned or killed, we *will* face problems as a result of our faith and our countercultural walk with God.

When you work for peace, show mercy to people who don't deserve it, thirst for things of God instead of possessions or success, and accept others without judgment and despite vast differences, not everyone will understand. Not everyone will like it. That goes for Christians and non-Christians alike. When your entire life is being transformed, you might lose some friends along the way.

But our attitude in the face of inevitable persecution is a choice that's determined by our focus in life. If we are focused on living like Jesus, we will continue to be content and to find joy. Just keep your eyes on Him and remember that you are never alone.

# WHERE ARE YOU?

*Have you ever been singled out or treated differently from others because of your faith?*

_____

_____

_____

_____

_____

*Is there anything wrong with wanting instant gratification?*

_____

_____

_____

_____

_____

*What are some ways that you keep from giving up on the promises of Jesus?*

_____

_____

_____

_____

_____

# A PRAYER

Jesus, thank You for reminding me that I am never alone. Give me the strength to continue on when others are cruel and it feels as though no one is there. Help me to remember that You have been through the same difficulties and even worse hardships. When I am uncertain, remind me that my strength is in You. In Your name, amen.

# DAY 69:
## RECOGNIZING OUR NEED

## SCRIPTURE READING

LUKE 6:24–26 (NIV)

> But woe to you who are rich,
> for you have already received your comfort.
> Woe to you who are well fed now,
> for you will go hungry.
> Woe to you who laugh now,
> for you will mourn and weep.
> Woe to you when everyone speaks well of you,
> for that is how their ancestors treated the false prophets.

## LIFE LESSONS

We live in a world that constantly tempts us to want things. Our culture urges us to buy more, to collect more, to upgrade, to get those shoes in multiple colors. It tells us that we always need more regardless of what we already have and that our wants are really needs. It advises us to seek success and popularity so we can start living the "ideal lifestyle."

It is easy for abundance and success to blind us to our true need for God—when we have all we want, why would we need Jesus? If we don't recognize that we are lacking, what part of us would we seek Him to fill?

In this passage, Jesus teaches us that blessings come to the poor because desperate people keep hungering for God. From this, it is easy to form a moral dichotomy that says wealth equates with separation from God, and poverty brings righteousness, but let's be clear: it is not wrong to have abundance. But if what we have is more important to us than our relationship and walk with Jesus, then it becomes a problem.

Our collections of possessions and wealth can be destroyed or taken from us at any time. But our relationship with Jesus is there to sustain us whether we are living comfortably or meagerly. We can sum it up by saying, "I would rather have nothing now and Jesus forever than have everything this world has to offer and miss out on Him."

## WHERE ARE YOU?

*How would you sum up Jesus's teaching in this passage in a sentence?*

_____

_____

_____

_____

_____

*What do you think of when you hear the word abundance?*

_____

_____

_____

_____

_____

*What are the possessions or things that get in the way of your relationship with Jesus?*

_____

_____

_____

_____

_____

## A PRAYER

Lord God, please help me not to lose my focus on You by chasing after material things and worldly success. If I am blessed with abundance, help me to use it wisely and not to lose sight of You. If I lose everything, help me to look to You for comfort and help. Let my focus continue to be an eternal perspective. In Your name, amen.

# DAY 70:
## SALT OF THE EARTH

## SCRIPTURE READING

**MATTHEW 5:13 (NIV)**

*You are the salt of the earth. But if the salt loses its saltiness, how can it be made salty again? It is no longer good for anything, except to be thrown out and trampled underfoot.*

## LIFE LESSONS

Salt is powerful. Anyone who has ever accidentally put a tablespoon instead of a teaspoon of salt into a baking dish can attest to that. Its flavor is intense. One little grain of salt is two thousand times more powerful than its size. That brings new perspective to God's calling us to be *"the salt of the earth,"* doesn't it?

The Romans regarded salt as a precious and vital commodity. In fact, the word "salary" comes from the word for "salt." A Roman soldier's salary was an allowance for purchasing salt; sometimes, soldiers were even paid in salt. This is where the phrase "not worth his salt" comes from. If a Roman soldier didn't do his job well, he didn't deserve his salt.

Salt permeates and flavors everything it touches, but it doesn't only add flavor, it also serves as a preservative. In biblical times there was no refrigeration, so salt's ability to keep food edible made it all the more valuable, as it saved food from going rotten.

All of these things that are true of salt are also true of a believer. When we walk with Jesus and come to know Him, this relationship permeates our lives, bringing His influence out into the world through the relationships we make and the people we interact with. It adds hope and love to a broken world. It also preserves His teachings and adds value to our lives and the lives of those around us.

# WHERE ARE YOU?

*What does the warning in this verse mean?*

_____

_____

_____

_____

*Would you say your faith walk is "salty" or "not salty"? Why?*

_____

_____

_____

_____

*In what ways can believers lose their saltiness?*

_____

_____

_____

_____

# A PRAYER

Dear Jesus, thank You for Your ability to look at a broken person like me and see my potential. I pray that I would be an example of You and Your love and grace for other people. Help me to never lose sight of the importance of this task. In Your name, amen.

# DAY 71:
## DRAWN BY THE LIGHT

## SCRIPTURE READING

MATTHEW 5:14–16 (NIV)

*You are the light of the world. A town built on a hill cannot be hidden. Neither do people light a lamp and put it under a bowl. Instead they put it on its stand, and it gives light to everyone in the house. In the same way, let your light shine before others, that they may see your good deeds and glorify your Father in heaven.*

## LIFE LESSONS

Light illuminates. It offers the hope of safety and refuge in dark times and dark places, pointing the way and helping us avoid danger. Light also penetrates, providing visibility and clarity. One small candle can light up an entire room, and a single light from a lighthouse can be seen from miles away by a ship seeking safe harbor.

Those who walk with Jesus are like a light in the darkness for those who need Him. Their lives will draw people in. Their lifestyle should serve as a poignant reminder of Jesus's promises. People naturally seek out light. They will naturally seek out the encouragement, the kind words, the grace and acceptance, the life you live when your life imitates Christ's.

Isolating yourself won't do anyone any good. Light isn't meant to be hidden. It's supposed to shine; it's supposed to be seen. We have to go out into the world and interact with people. When we do, Jesus's light will shine through us. People will be drawn to Him through us.

## WHERE ARE YOU?

*In your own words, how are believers "the light of the world"?*

_____

_____

_____

_____

_____

*What holds you back from being a light to others at times?*

_____

_____

_____

_____

_____

*What good deeds have you seen shining light into a dark world recently?*

_____

_____

_____

_____

_____

## A PRAYER

Jesus, help me to be salt and light to this world so that others may see You and find You as well. Let my life be one that draws people in. Help my salt to never lose its flavor, and help my light to shine brightly in a dark world. In Your name, amen.

# DAY 72:
## OUR INABILITY BUT HIS CAPABILITY

## SCRIPTURE READING

MATTHEW 5:17–20 (NIV)

*Do not think that I have come to abolish the Law or the Prophets; I have not come to abolish them but to fulfill them. For truly I tell you, until heaven and earth disappear, not the smallest letter, not the least stroke of a pen, will by any means disappear from the Law until everything is accomplished. Therefore anyone who sets aside one of the least of these commands and teaches others accordingly will be called least in the kingdom of heaven, but whoever practices and teaches these commands will be called great in the kingdom of heaven. For I tell you that unless your righteousness surpasses that of the Pharisees and the teachers of the law, you will certainly not enter the kingdom of heaven.*

## LIFE LESSONS

When Jesus began His earthly ministry, many people questioned if His teachings meant that He planned to cancel the law established in the Scriptures—was He going to disregard the Law and the Prophets? This was a large part of why His words angered so many. They didn't understand (and many didn't want to).

Jesus clarified that He had not come to abolish the law but to fulfill it because we couldn't do so on our own. We couldn't live up to the requirements of the law, regardless of how hard we tried.

Jesus was the only perfect person to ever walk on this earth. He kept the commandments of His Father perfectly. While the law points out *our* inability to keep God's commandments and *our* need for a Savior, those very same commandments also point us to Jesus. Jesus made a way for us to enter heaven when He fulfilled those commandments Himself and sacrificed Himself for us.

## WHERE ARE YOU?

*What did Jesus mean when He said that He had come to "fulfill" the Law and the Prophets?*

_____

_____

_____

_____

*How can our righteousness "[surpass] that of the Pharisees and the teachers of the law"?*

_____

_____

_____

_____

*As you read today's Scripture passage, what promise stood out to you?*

_____

_____

_____

_____

## A PRAYER

Jesus, thank You for coming and fulfilling the law when we couldn't live up to it on our own. No matter how hard I try to obey, I'm reminded that I need You. I am weak and imperfect, but You are strong. You love me regardless and are here for me regardless. Thank You for that. In Your name, amen.

# DAY 73:
## THE ATTITUDE BEHIND THE ACTION

## SCRIPTURE READING

### MATTHEW 5:21–22 (NIV)

*You have heard that it was said to the people long ago, "You shall not murder, and anyone who murders will be subject to judgment." But I tell you that anyone who is angry with a brother or sister will be subject to judgment. Again, anyone who says to a brother or sister, "Raca," is answerable to the court. And anyone who says, "You fool!" will be in danger of the fire of hell.*

## LIFE LESSONS

Don't panic! Jesus's teaching in this passage sounds extreme, but behind the initial shock of His words is a solid and beneficial point that is meant to help us on our journey, not condemn us.

In Matthew 5, Jesus gives a series of statements that all begin with the phrase *"You have heard"* and go on to say, *"But I tell you…."* Basically, He is emphasizing that the Old Testament law has a deeper meaning than what most people understood. People had come to focus on the action of the law, but Jesus points to the attitude behind the action.

The law of the Old Testament took on a whole new standard with Jesus. He got to the heart of the matter because it is a matter of the heart. Jesus revealed the importance of our thoughts. That's where everything starts and begins to grow in us, influencing who we are. Wrong thoughts can lead to wrong actions. Letting certain thoughts simmer can lead to dwelling on them, the development of worse thoughts, the establishment of an accompanying attitude or viewpoint, and then an action or lifestyle that can hurt us or someone else.

We need to keep an eye on the small things because they can become big. This is why spending time with Jesus to maintain a pure heart is so important.

## WHERE ARE YOU?

*With whom have you been angry or experienced conflict lately?*

_____

_____

_____

_____

_____

*Have you sought reconciliation with this individual? If not, what might be the first steps to doing so?*

_____

_____

_____

_____

_____

*Consider whether you are harboring any anger in your heart. If you are, what steps can you take to let that anger go?*

_____

_____

_____

_____

_____

## A PRAYER

Jesus, thank You for reminding me that my attitude is just as important as my actions. Help me to not harbor anger in my heart and to keep my thoughts pure and loving. I pray that Your love would flow through me so that I can unconditionally love others. In Your name, amen.

# DAY 74:
## THE BARRIER OF BROKEN RELATIONSHIPS

## SCRIPTURE READING

MATTHEW 5:23–26 (NIV)

*Therefore, if you are offering your gift at the altar and there remember that your brother or sister has something against you, leave your gift there in front of the altar. First go and be reconciled to them; then come and offer your gift.*

*Settle matters quickly with your adversary who is taking you to court. Do it while you are still together on the way, or your adversary may hand you over to the judge, and the judge may hand you over to the officer, and you may be thrown into prison. Truly I tell you, you will not get out until you have paid the last penny.*

## LIFE LESSONS

God calls us to not hold on to anger. It gets in the way of our walk with Him, and it can lead us down roads we really don't want to take. Anger is volatile, and resentment can grow easily, making situations worse. And, perhaps worst of all, anger keeps us from giving everything to God. If we try to worship God with anger and hatred in our heart toward others, we can't fully absorb the guidance we need. We're not fully taking Him in. It creates a barrier.

Anger is the enemy of relationship, and relationship is the central component of walking with Jesus. Why else would Jesus have taught that the greatest commandments are to love Him and love others? (See Matthew 22:36–40.) Broken relationships eat at the very essence of our peace, and this can affect our relationship with Jesus and our relationships with those around us.

A critical issue in today's broken and divided world is the disparity in the message from those who claim to love Jesus but show in their actions that they do not love others, especially if those others are not like them. If we cannot love like Jesus, do we really love Him?

# WHERE ARE YOU?

*How would you summarize this lesson in your own words?*

_____
_____
_____
_____
_____

*In these verses, what change is Jesus calling us to make?*

_____
_____
_____
_____

*In what ways can anger interfere with relationships?*

_____
_____
_____
_____

# A PRAYER

Jesus, I pray that I would love like You, that my words and actions would always match up. When I have a strained relationship with someone, give me the strength to humble myself, forgive, and seek restoration with the person, whether I have wronged them or they have wronged me. In Your name, amen.

## DAY 75:
## FEEDING OUR THOUGHTS FOR THE BETTER

## SCRIPTURE READING

### MATTHEW 5:27–30 (NIV)

*You have heard that it was said, "You shall not commit adultery." But I tell you that anyone who looks at a woman lustfully has already committed adultery with her in his heart. If your right eye causes you to stumble, gouge it out and throw it away. It is better for you to lose one part of your body than for your whole body to be thrown into hell. And if your right hand causes you to stumble, cut it off and throw it away. It is better for you to lose one part of your body than for your whole body to go into hell.*

## LIFE LESSONS

Here, once again, Jesus takes the existing law and puts it into a new context: we need to control what happens in our hearts and minds before the opportunity to commit sin arrives on our doorstep. If the opportunity is something we've been bent on for a while, the thought we've been feeding ourselves, it can be hard to say no when it's right in front of us.

This isn't a rule just to be a rule. It protects us and others from severe and far-reaching consequences. In this day and age, who hasn't seen the consequences of infidelity? Infidelity can lead to ruined careers, separated households, broken communities, lost friends, and irreconcilable relationships. It leaves people in confusion and despair.

Jesus emphasizes that what is in our heart reveals where we are in our walk as much as our actions do. Our mindset is equally as important as our actions. If we think it, we are likely to do it.

Today, we have far too many opportunities to prepare ourselves for our own downfall. Our phones and computers give us easy access to potentially wrong people and a firehose of thoughts that don't align with Jesus's teachings. They can take us to unhealthy spaces, causing us to dwell on the desires of the world at the expense of the lives we've built. It's crucial that we remain aware of what we're taking in, that we guard our thoughts, and that we regularly realign our hearts and minds with Jesus.

## WHERE ARE YOU?

*Have you allowed social media to negatively shape your perspective on a moral issue?*

_____

_____

_____

_____

_____

*Would you say that the things you routinely read and watch reflect your heart?*

_____

_____

_____

_____

_____

*How might you be more discerning in the things that you allow to shape your heart?*

_____

_____

_____

_____

_____

## A PRAYER

Jesus, I pray that I would be diligent in feeding my heart beneficial things, positive things, that are of You. I recognize that my thoughts and actions don't always reflect You and Your ways. Thank You for Your grace and mercy. Help me to be aware of my thoughts and to keep my eyes on You. In Your name, amen.

# DAY 76:
## SHOWING UP TO CARE AND SACRIFICE

## SCRIPTURE READING

MATTHEW 5:31–32 (NIV)

*It has been said, "Anyone who divorces his wife must give her a certificate of divorce." But I tell you that anyone who divorces his wife, except for sexual immorality, makes her the victim of adultery, and anyone who marries a divorced woman commits adultery.*

## LIFE LESSONS

The only biblically approved cause for divorce is unfaithfulness. However, the concept of "faithfulness" is much broader than just sexual fidelity. At the core of unfaithfulness is a broken relationship, which can have many causes.

A successful marriage requires that both spouses constantly show up to do the work. The marital relationship is meant to imitate our relationship with Jesus. In Ephesians 5:25–33, Paul describes marriage as an illustration of the way Christ and the church are one, meaning that marriage is meant to demonstrate how God loves His people. There is no end to what God will do for His people. He is always there, loving us through the hard times, forgiving us when we fall. A healthy marriage should reflect the same level of care and sacrifice.

## WHERE ARE YOU?

*How does the marital relationship mirror our relationship with Jesus?*

_____

_____

_____

_____

_____

*Describe a time when you witnessed a husband and wife demonstrate unconditional love to the world.*

_____

_____

_____

_____

*If you are married, what might you do to better "show up to do the work" of your marriage?*

_____

_____

_____

_____

_____

## A PRAYER

God, thank You for providing the opportunity for an incredible connection between two people through marriage. Give me the patience and strength to show up in all my relationships and put in the work to make them healthy and strong. Let my relationships demonstrate pure love to others as a reflection of Your love for us. In Jesus's name, amen.

**DAY 77:**
# NO SECOND-GUESSING, NOTHING TO PROVE

## SCRIPTURE READING

MATTHEW 5:33–37 (NIV)

*Again, you have heard that it was said to the people long ago, "Do not break your oath, but fulfill to the Lord the vows you have made." But I tell you, do not swear an oath at all: either by heaven, for it is God's throne; or by the earth, for it is his footstool; or by Jerusalem, for it is the city of the Great King. And do not swear by your head, for you cannot make even one hair white or black. All you need to say is simply "Yes" or "No"; anything beyond this comes from the evil one.*

## LIFE LESSONS

The last time someone adamantly swore to you that this time around would be different, what was your first thought? Probably not, "I believe you!" It was probably more along the lines of, "We'll see."

Honest people have nothing to prove. They don't have to worry because they have nothing to hide—no made-up stories they must keep straight, no guilt urging them to cover their tracks, no reason to swear on their life that some task will get done or that they weren't responsible for a certain mistake. When you keep your word, you never have to swear your honesty to anyone to try to prove the authenticity of your answer.

Jesus says we should be people of our word. A trustworthy person always says what they mean and always means what they say. No one should have to wonder or second-guess when they ask us a question or when we tell them we'll do something.

## WHERE ARE YOU?

*What are some "little white lies" you've heard yourself tell?*

_____

_____

_____

_____

_____

*Have you ever had to admit to having told a lie to someone?*

_____

_____

_____

_____

*How do you feel when you've discovered someone close to you has been dishonest with you?*

_____

_____

_____

_____

_____

## A PRAYER

Jesus, I pray that I would be known as an authentic, honest person. Help me to do what I say I am going to do. Help me to be a person of my word whom others can trust and count on. In Your name, amen.

# DAY 78:
## A PATH OF RECONCILIATION

## SCRIPTURE READING

MATTHEW 5:38–42 (NIV)

*You have heard that it was said, "Eye for eye, and tooth for tooth." But I tell you, do not resist an evil person. If anyone slaps you on the right cheek, turn to them the other cheek also. And if anyone wants to sue you and take your shirt, hand over your coat as well. If anyone forces you to go one mile, go with them two miles. Give to the one who asks you, and do not turn away from the one who wants to borrow from you.*

SEE ALSO: LUKE 6:29–30

## LIFE LESSONS

In Jesus's time, a Roman soldier could force a Jew to carry his supplies one mile. The Jews would count the steps until they carried the items one mile and then would not take one step farther. Jesus teaches that we shouldn't count our steps—we should keep going. He calls us to exemplify His servant heart by doing more than is expected of us. In the face of both real and perceived wrongs, we should choose the path of peace and reconciliation.

It's important to recognize that, in these verses, Jesus is not calling us to accept criminal assault or domestic abuse. Take care of yourself! When necessary, leave bad situations and let the police and the courts do their jobs. That's an issue of protecting both yourself and your community. Just be sure that if you *are* reporting someone or bringing consequences of some kind down on their head, whether it's for something large or small, do so with pure motivations, not driven by malice. No circumstances should turn you from continuing to show God's love.

Even when we are hurting or frustrated, we are still an example to others. Even when our circumstances are unfair, instead of looking for revenge, we should be looking for opportunities to show the unconditional love of Jesus.

## WHERE ARE YOU?

*When have you experienced a situation in which you had to "turn the other cheek"?*

_____

_____

_____

_____

*In practical terms, what is Jesus calling us to do in these verses?*

_____

_____

_____

_____

*What are some possible indicators that you are acting out of malice or revenge instead of showing God's love?*

_____

_____

_____

_____

_____

## A PRAYER

Jesus, I know that I am always an example to others, whether I want to be or not. I pray that I wouldn't let my emotions run away with me when I'm upset or angry. Seeing the potential for good in every situation can be difficult for me. Help me to never be vengeful but to view others the same way You see them. Keep me gracious and understanding. In Your name, amen.

# DAY 79:
## LOVING REGARDLESS

## SCRIPTURE READING

MATTHEW 5:43–48 (NIV)

*You have heard that it was said, "Love your neighbor and hate your enemy." But I tell you, love your enemies and pray for those who persecute you, that you may be children of your Father in heaven. He causes his sun to rise on the evil and the good, and sends rain on the righteous and the unrighteous. If you love those who love you, what reward will you get? Are not even the tax collectors doing that? And if you greet only your own people, what are you doing more than others? Do not even pagans do that? Be perfect, therefore, as your heavenly Father is perfect.*

SEE ALSO: LUKE 6:27–28, 32–36

## LIFE LESSONS

It's easy to love people who look like us, think like us, and love us in return. Anyone can do that. It's much harder to love those who are mean to us—people who have hurt us or treated us cruelly. Sometimes we don't even realize how we treat people when we dislike them or carry around our anger toward them.

Jesus calls us to love our enemies and to do good to those who wish us ill. To the rest of the world, loving everyone, regardless of what they've done to us, may seem naive, a sign of weakness. But if we are walking with Jesus, our journey will be different. We will be different. If we are seeking to love like Jesus, we conform to a different set of values—and that might make us seem odd or backward to the people around us. We might be told we're fighting a losing battle for continuing to show love to someone, but it doesn't matter. God wants us to love that person, to show patience and compassion. (Again, loving someone does not mean staying in a dangerous environment. If you are experiencing physical or emotional abuse in a relationship, you need to protect yourself, set boundaries, and consult a trained counselor right away.)

When we are walking with Jesus, we know God's unconditional love. By loving those who hate us, we show the very nature of our Father in heaven. Choosing this journey means we are committed to demonstrating God's love to *all*.

## WHERE ARE YOU?

*How do you feel when you read these verses out loud?*

_____

_____

_____

_____

_____

*Whom do you find hardest to love?*

_____

_____

_____

_____

_____

*How can you change your heart from disliking someone to loving them?*

_____

_____

_____

_____

_____

## A PRAYER

Dear Jesus, thank You for loving me unconditionally with Your boundless grace and mercy. Thank You for blessing me in ways that I never could have imagined. I ask that You would work through my life so that others can experience the same love. Help me to love the people who've hurt me, no matter what the rest of the world thinks. In Your name, amen.

# DAY 80:
## MOTIVES OF A PURE HEART

## SCRIPTURE READING

### MATTHEW 6:1–4 (NIV)

*Be careful not to practice your righteousness in front of others to be seen by them. If you do, you will have no reward from your Father in heaven.*

*So when you give to the needy, do not announce it with trumpets, as the hypocrites do in the synagogues and on the streets, to be honored by others. Truly I tell you, they have received their reward in full. But when you give to the needy, do not let your left hand know what your right hand is doing, so that your giving may be in secret. Then your Father, who sees what is done in secret, will reward you.*

## LIFE LESSONS

At some point, all of us have probably done something good just for the praise we would receive. Being praised feels good. It's normal to want recognition when we do good—when we're generous, kind, or effusive in our praise of someone else. So why is Jesus telling us to keep our good deeds private?

This teaching is not about hiding *everything* we do from other people. After all, Jesus tells us to demonstrate His love through our actions, to shine like a city on a hill (see Matthew 5:14–15), and we can't do that when we act in secret. He's talking about the motivations behind our actions. Our motivation for doing good shouldn't be receiving praise or attention. We shouldn't stand up to brag about the things we've done or choose to do something charitable only if our name will show up on the list of donors. If recognition is why we're doing something nice, the only reward will be the approval of the people around us. If we did it just for the admiration of others, then we've already won what we were seeking. It's over. There's nothing more.

This is about our attitude and our approach to loving others. When we do good things to show off God's love, we become more like Him, we genuinely help people, and we are rewarded by God. We should be motivated to give as Jesus gave: freely and without expectation. We should give with a pure heart.

## WHERE ARE YOU?

*Have you ever given money or volunteered to do something because you thought it would make you look good?*

_____

_____

_____

_____

_____

*Where does the real reward come from when we give to others?*

_____

_____

_____

_____

_____

*What good deed could you do in private to show your love for Jesus?*

_____

_____

_____

_____

_____

## A PRAYER

Jesus, please purify the motives of my heart. Teach me to give like You gave, with a pure heart and without expectation. I pray that I would serve You and others with a humble heart each day. In Your name, amen.

# DAY 81:
## PRAYERS FROM THE HEART

## SCRIPTURE READING

### MATTHEW 6:5–8 (NIV)

*And when you pray, do not be like the hypocrites, for they love to pray standing in the synagogues and on the street corners to be seen by others. Truly I tell you, they have received their reward in full. But when you pray, go into your room, close the door and pray to your Father, who is unseen. Then your Father, who sees what is done in secret, will reward you. And when you pray, do not keep on babbling like pagans, for they think they will be heard because of their many words. Do not be like them, for your Father knows what you need before you ask him.*

## LIFE LESSONS

In biblical times, *hypocrite* was a term used for a playactor in a theatrical production. It's not surprising that Jesus used this concept when He described people who aren't honest in their communication with God. One of the easiest places to play a hypocrite before God is in our prayer lives.

If we're praying in a public place, we may find ourselves speaking in a certain manner or saying things simply to impress those around us. Or, if we're not careful, we might fall into rote prayers based on routine rather than a personal relationship with Jesus. God deserves genuine prayer from His children. When we have a conversation with a close friend, do we want a scripted dialogue? Of course not. Do we want them to change their words to impress the people around us? Not at all. We want our friend to be responsive and interactive and to focus on our conversation.

Jesus desires no less. He wants to know what we are thinking and feeling. He wishes for us to tell Him, not because He needs the information, but because when we tell Him, we make it real for ourselves. He knows everything, and He knows if we're being genuine or just playing a part.

## WHERE ARE YOU?

*What are some of the things you have been praying for lately?*

_____
_____
_____
_____
_____

*What are the things you are most thankful for today?*

_____
_____
_____
_____
_____

*Who are the people you have been praying for?*

_____
_____
_____
_____
_____

## A PRAYER

Lord, thank You for the gift of prayer. Thank You for offering us a direct connection with You and a personal relationship with You. Thank You that, today and every day, I can come to You with anything and know You are with me, listening. Help me to rely on You in all things. In Your name, amen.

# DAY 82:
## BLUEPRINTS FOR PRAYER

## SCRIPTURE READING

MATTHEW 6:9–15 (NIV)

*This, then, is how you should pray:*

*"Our Father in heaven,*

*hallowed be your name,*

*your kingdom come,*

*your will be done,*

  *on earth as it is in heaven.*

*Give us today our daily bread.*

*And forgive us our debts,*

  *as we also have forgiven our debtors.*

*And lead us not into temptation,*

  *but deliver us from the evil one."*

*For if you forgive other people when they sin against you, your heavenly Father will also forgive you. But if you do not forgive others their sins, your Father will not forgive your sins.*

## LIFE LESSONS

In this passage, Jesus is not talking in terms of *if* we pray; He is teaching about *when* we pray. Jesus expects us to spend daily time with Him. However, our prayers are not measured by quantity but by the motives of our hearts. God desires quality—genuine time with Him.

Many of us grew up reciting the Lord's Prayer from memory. Few of us received it as a model for our prayer life, but that is how Jesus intended it. He instructed that we "pray like this," and then gave a sample prayer that includes praise, priority, provisions, pardon, and protection.

We all have days when we get before God and nothing comes out. Our mind goes blank. When we feel stuck or aren't sure where to start, this prayer serves as a guide. Sometimes it can just get us going. Pulling out this prayer can draw us closer to real conversation with Jesus when we don't have the words.

# WHERE ARE YOU?

*In what way is the Lord's Prayer a template for your own prayers?*

_____

_____

_____

_____

_____

*Which component of the Lord's Prayer—praise, priority, provisions, pardon, or protection—is the hardest for you to include in your prayers? Why do you think this is so?*

_____

_____

_____

_____

*If you could make a change to your prayer life, what would it look like?*

_____

_____

_____

_____

_____

# A PRAYER

Lord Jesus, Thank You for providing the words when I don't have them. I know You desire words from the heart—to hear my hopes, my fears, my praise, my everyday frustrations, *everything*. I want to be comfortable in Your presence. Please guide me every day into a deeper and more meaningful relationship with You. In Your name, amen.

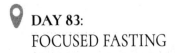 **DAY 83:**
FOCUSED FASTING

## SCRIPTURE READING

MATTHEW 6:16–18 (NLT)

*And when you fast, don't make it obvious, as the hypocrites do, for they try to look miserable and disheveled so people will admire them for their fasting. I tell you the truth, that is the only reward they will ever get. But when you fast, comb your hair and wash your face. Then no one will notice that you are fasting, except your Father, who knows what you do in private. And your Father, who sees everything, will reward you.*

## LIFE LESSONS

When hypocrites fast, they make sure that everyone knows what they're doing and how difficult it is. But fasting was never meant to be a public display of religion. It isn't supposed to be for demonstration but for transformation. The purpose of fasting is to draw us closer to God and further into His presence, to deepen our relationship with Him.

The act of fasting takes away negative elements that are lingering between us and God or things we heavily rely on, forcing us to depend even more on Him. The *results* of fasting should be revealed through our lives, while the *act* of fasting should remain a secret in our hearts. The reward of fasting is a deeper relationship with God.

Here Jesus continues to focus on attitude, action, and motivations. Again, He mentions that doing something for public admiration provides only that temporary reward—some brief recognition that won't matter in the long run. Our reward should be our relationship with Jesus, not the recognition of others.

## WHERE ARE YOU?

*Have you ever participated in the spiritual discipline of fasting? If so, what was it like?*

_____

_____

_____

_____

*What are some barriers between you and God that the act of fasting could help to remove?*

_____

_____

_____

_____

*If you were to try fasting now, in order to improve your journey with Jesus, what kind of fast might you participate in? Be sure to start slowly, especially if you have never fasted before, and follow healthy guidelines.*

_____

_____

_____

_____

## A PRAYER

Jesus, thank You for providing so many ways for me to draw closer to You. I pray that on my journey, it wouldn't be about what others see externally but what You see internally. Keep my heart humble and my motives pure. In Your name, amen.

**DAY 84:**
## TREASURING OUR TREASURES

## SCRIPTURE READING

MATTHEW 6:19–21 (NLT)

*Don't store up treasures here on earth, where moths eat them and rust destroys them, and where thieves break in and steal. Store your treasures in heaven, where moths and rust cannot destroy, and thieves do not break in and steal. Wherever your treasure is, there the desires of your heart will also be.*

## LIFE LESSONS

In today's world, people are often measured by their possessions. The car, the house, the clothes, the schools the kids attend—these elements and more are used to determine an individual's worth. Consequently, we start finding our worth in our possessions, and we continue amassing them.

The Greek word for *"store up"* gives us our English word *thesaurus*. A thesaurus is a treasury of words. With this in mind, we could also translate Jesus's teaching here as, "Do not treasure your treasures."

As we've established before, there is nothing inherently wrong with having things. We are going to have possessions. We'll even have possessions that we really care for or appreciate. And, of course, we want to work hard to provide the best for ourselves and our families. The problem isn't in having things; the problem comes when our things "have" us. When seeking out possessions for a certain lifestyle, being able to buy more and more, and possibly hoarding possessions, take precedence over our walk with God.

God warns us to be careful of what we consider most important. If the things we have are more important to us than walking with Jesus, loving our families, and loving others as we love ourselves, then we show where our heart really lies.

## WHERE ARE YOU?

*If your house were to catch fire, what item(s) would you grab to preserve as you ran for safety?*

_____

_____

_____

_____

_____

*How do our possessions reflect our desires?*

_____

_____

_____

_____

_____

*What would you say is the greatest treasure in your life?*

_____

_____

_____

_____

_____

## A PRAYER

Father, thank You for being the Lord of my heart. Help me to treasure You more than anything else in my life. May my focus be on You. Help me view my relationship with You as my greatest possession. In Jesus's name, amen.

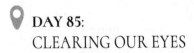

# DAY 85:
# CLEARING OUR EYES

## SCRIPTURE READING

MATTHEW 6:22–23 (NIV)

*The eye is the lamp of the body. If your eyes are healthy, your whole body will be full of light. But if your eyes are unhealthy, your whole body will be full of darkness. If then the light within you is darkness, how great is that darkness!*

## LIFE LESSONS

When a window in a room is clean and the glass is clear, sunlight can directly enter every part of the room. When a window is dirty, the light can't shine through, and the room will be dim. The quantity and quality of the light that shines into a room from outside depends entirely on the window through which it comes. Jesus's analogy here is clear (pardon the pun): if our eyes are "the windows of the soul," then the light that comes into our soul directly depends on the condition of our spiritual eyes.

Jesus utters these words as part of His teachings about money and possessions. When we focus primarily on temporary aspirations (or worldly aspirations), like hoarding money, it clouds our view of God. We become greedy and put our own selfish interests first. We lose sight of God and what it means to honor Him. This makes it difficult for us to pursue truth, patience, humility, and other important facets of our walk with Jesus. When we refocus on Him and our spiritual eyesight is clear, His light will be within us so it can shine through us.

## WHERE ARE YOU?

*Where do you see spiritual darkness as being most prevalent in our world?*

_____

_____

_____

_____

_____

*What can a believer do to have their spiritual eyes opened?*

_____

_____

_____

_____

_____

*In this Scripture passage, Jesus again referenced "light." What do spiritual maturity and light have in common?*

_____

_____

_____

_____

_____

## A PRAYER

Jesus, keep my eyes clear and focused on You so I can be filled with Your light and love. I pray for strength against greed and a renewed energy every day to continue seeking after You. In Your name, amen.

## DAY 86:
## MASTERING MONEY

## SCRIPTURE READING

MATTHEW 6:24 (NIV)

*No one can serve two masters. Either you will hate the one and love the other, or you will be devoted to the one and despise the other. You cannot serve both God and money.*

## LIFE LESSONS

It is impossible to have two masters. They will, without a doubt, be in conflict as each tries to direct your actions, decisions, and responses to situations. You can't cater to both masters all the time. At some point, they will ask different things of you, and you will have to decide which one you're going to obey.

Jesus doesn't say, "You *should* not" or "You *must* not serve God and money." Jesus clearly tells us that we *cannot* serve both. There is no way to do it.

We all need money to survive, and we want to be able to provide abundantly for ourselves and for our families. The issue arises when our efforts to earn and accumulate money begin to control our lives. When we make decisions according to our bank account, regardless of the effect it may have on our spiritual walk, our money has started to control us.

Money can easily end up controlling our lives. But there is room in our hearts for only one master, and only one of them loves you unconditionally.

## WHERE ARE YOU?

*In what ways can money control us?*

_____

_____

_____

_____

_____

*When has money become a barrier to your spiritual life?*

_____

_____

_____

_____

_____

*How can you prioritize earning and spending in a way that reflects and reinforces your journey with Jesus?*

_____

_____

_____

_____

_____

## A PRAYER

Lord Jesus, thank You for reminding us that we can't have it both ways. There will be times when we have to choose, and I pray that I would always make You my first priority, no matter how tempting anything else may seem. Please give me the strength and clear-headedness to make the right choice. In Your name, amen.

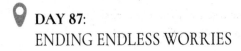

# DAY 87:
## ENDING ENDLESS WORRIES

## SCRIPTURE READING

MATTHEW 6:25–34 (NIV)

*Therefore I tell you, do not worry about your life, what you will eat or drink; or about your body, what you will wear. Is not life more than food, and the body more than clothes? Look at the birds of the air; they do not sow or reap or store away in barns, and yet your heavenly Father feeds them. Are you not much more valuable than they? Can any one of you by worrying add a single hour to your life?*

*And why do you worry about clothes? See how the flowers of the field grow. They do not labor or spin. Yet I tell you that not even Solomon in all his splendor was dressed like one of these. If that is how God clothes the grass of the field, which is here today and tomorrow is thrown into the fire, will he not much more clothe you—you of little faith? So do not worry, saying, "What shall we eat?" or "What shall we drink?" or "What shall we wear?" For the pagans run after all these things, and your heavenly Father knows that you need them. But seek first his kingdom and his righteousness, and all these things will be given to you as well. Therefore do not worry about tomorrow, for tomorrow will worry about itself. Each day has enough trouble of its own.*

## LIFE LESSONS

Worrying. Some of us do it more than others, but we all fall prey to it at times. We can worry about pretty much anything: the next rent check, our health, that presentation coming up, that deadline, our future, whether our child or parent will get sick.

Jesus's teaching about worry is timeless. Even though He delivered it long, long ago, the lesson still fits today. Jesus addresses a few major categories of worry: finances, food, fashion, and the future. These four areas can keep us up at night. Granted, a certain level of *concern* for these areas is actually productive. If we're never concerned, we might get lazy and fail to act when necessary. Worry becomes problematic when we're already doing what we can, but we're still stressing out trying to solve the unsolvable. In this case, the root of worry is a lack of faith. Faith and worry cannot coexist. Either we trust God, or we worry about life. So, to worry less, we have to trust God more.

God *will* come through. If you're holding up your end, have faith that God will hold up His. Have faith in His plan for you. This is much more easily said than done, but our peace comes with listening and trusting. It comes with faith.

## WHERE ARE YOU?

*As you reflect on these verses, think about which area of your life keeps you awake at night the most often.*

_____

_____

_____

_____

_____

*If someone came to you to talk through their worries, what encouragement from Scripture and practical advice might you give them?*

_____

_____

_____

_____

*How can faith in Jesus help us understand how to let go of fears and begin to trust in God?*

_____

_____

_____

_____

_____

## A PRAYER

Father, I don't want to spend countless hours worrying when You've already told me not to worry. Give me faith to trust You more. When worries arise, help me put my confidence in You and Your plan for me. I know You are more than able to handle anything that comes my way. In Jesus's name, amen.

# DAY 88:
## FOCUSING ON OURSELVES FIRST

## SCRIPTURE READING

MATTHEW 7:1–6 (NLT)

*Do not judge others, and you will not be judged. For you will be treated as you treat others. The standard you use in judging is the standard by which you will be judged.*

*And why worry about a speck in your friend's eye when you have a log in your own? How can you think of saying to your friend, "Let me help you get rid of that speck in your eye," when you can't see past the log in your own eye? Hypocrite! First get rid of the log in your own eye; then you will see well enough to deal with the speck in your friend's eye.*

*Don't waste what is holy on people who are unholy. Don't throw your pearls to pigs! They will trample the pearls, then turn and attack you.*

SEE ALSO: LUKE 6:37–42

## LIFE LESSONS

A wise person once said, "Don't point your finger at others, because when you do, there are three fingers pointing back at you." Nobody likes a critic who is always finding fault with others. We are *all* fallible, fallen people—there is plenty to criticize across the board. We all make mistakes and have shortcomings. We are all in need of grace.

Jesus cautions us against judging others. Other people have their own paths. We shouldn't be out there evaluating their every move. We should be looking at our own shortcomings and taking care of our own issues. If we're judging the people around us, we already have an issue we need to take care of: we're not focusing on God because we're too busy focusing on others. We need to examine our own lives and our own walk with Jesus first.

Once we've cleaned up our own issues, we begin to properly see God's priorities again. The more clearly we're able to see God's priorities, the less likely we are to fall into the trap of judging others. Instead, we're much more likely to encourage, to love, to genuinely help people instead of pointing out their faults.

## WHERE ARE YOU?

*When have you found yourself judging someone and failing to see your own errors?*

_____

_____

_____

_____

_____

*The church is often accused of being filled with hypocrites. In your experience, is that a fair judgment?*

_____

_____

_____

_____

_____

*In your own words, what does that last verse mean when it talks about pigs trampling pearls?*

_____

_____

_____

_____

_____

## A PRAYER

Jesus, help me to focus on You and not what other people are doing. Help me to see myself clearly so I can work to see You clearly. When it is needed, please let Your Spirit speak through me so I can speak the truth to others in love. In Your name, amen.

# DAY 89:
## ASK AWAY

## SCRIPTURE READING

MATTHEW 7:7–11 (NIV)

*Ask and it will be given to you; seek and you will find; knock and the door will be opened to you. For everyone who asks receives; the one who seeks finds; and to the one who knocks, the door will be opened.*

*Which of you, if your son asks for bread, will give him a stone? Or if he asks for a fish, will give him a snake? If you, then, though you are evil, know how to give good gifts to your children, how much more will your Father in heaven give good gifts to those who ask him!*

## LIFE LESSONS

If you're a parent, you know what it's like to have a child who just keeps on asking for something. In many cases, their persistence pays off because you either finally get tired of hearing their pleas or get excited about making their dreams come true. It is similar in our relationship with our heavenly Father. God is loving. He has a tenderness, a soft spot, for His children when we call on Him and when we keep coming back.

God wants us to ask Him for things, whether things we need or things we want. We are His children, and He is never too busy to listen to our requests, no matter how large or small. Our asking is never an inconvenience to Him. It doesn't matter how many times we ask—God never considers us a nuisance. God wants us to be persistent, to really try.

Jesus tells us to ask, to seek, to knock—to go about it in every way we can. In the original language, all three verbs are in the imperative tense, meaning they're all commands. Jesus *commands* us to pray and ask with determination.

The other side of this, though, is that God will respond, but He may not give you what you expected or what you thought you wanted. His version of a "good" gift may differ from yours—at least right now. Sometimes we don't yet have the wisdom to recognize that something is good. God, on the other hand, knows what is good for us, and He has our best interests at heart. So keep asking, keep pushing, keep entering His presence to ask Him for gifts, because He will come through, and He wants to bless you.

## WHERE ARE YOU?

*How do you perceive the heavenly Father: as a giver of good gifts or as something else?*

_____

_____

_____

_____

_____

*What are you asking the Lord for right now?*

_____

_____

_____

_____

_____

*How would you explain the concept of asking and receiving, or seeking and finding, to the person who says they have asked but have not received?*

_____

_____

_____

_____

_____

## A PRAYER

Lord Jesus, You never tire of me, and You want me to be persistent in asking for things. Thank You for loving me so much. Thank You for Your gifts and for always wanting to listen to me. Help me to never be afraid to ask for what I need, and give me understanding when Your answer is not what I expected. In Your name, amen.

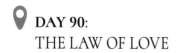

# DAY 90:
## THE LAW OF LOVE

## SCRIPTURE READINGS

MATTHEW 7:12 (NLT)

*Do to others whatever you would like them to do to you. This is the essence of all that is taught in the law and the prophets.*

LUKE 6:31 (NLT)

*Do to others as you would like them to do to you.*

## LIFE LESSONS

Notice that Jesus does not say, "Do to others whatever they did to you." He also does not say, "Do this to others so they will do something for you." He says, *"Do to others whatever you would like them to do to you."* In other words, act with love and kindness, having the other person's best interests at heart.

Jesus takes this principle to another level entirely when He adds, *"This is the essence of all that is taught in the law and the prophets."* With this, He is saying that the essence of everything that has been taught in the Scriptures for all time—what it all comes down to—is loving people. It's being kind and treating them well, wanting the best for them. That is to be at the core of everything we do. The old laws were about rules; the new laws are about relationships and how we love one another.

Human beings are selfish. We are prone to think more about ourselves than others. We want to do what we like and make ourselves happy, sometimes at others' expense. Walking with Jesus, however, gives us a new nature. We become like Him.

Jesus loves us fully, generously, relentlessly, endlessly. His love doesn't discriminate, and no matter what we do, He won't stop loving us. He puts us first. When we commit to *love Jesus* and *love like Jesus*, we gain the power to live our lives as we are called to live them.

## WHERE ARE YOU?

*When is it hardest to treat other people the way you want to be treated?*

_____
_____
_____
_____
_____

*Are there certain people with whom you have difficulty identifying?*

_____
_____
_____
_____
_____

*What can you do today to take a positive step toward treating others the way you want to be treated?*

_____
_____
_____
_____
_____

## A PRAYER

Dear Jesus, thank You for teaching us how to love people with our actions. Thank You for Your wise words and the incredible example of Your love. I pray that when people see me, they would see You. Help me to keep seeking You. In Your name, amen.

# CONCLUSION

Y ou did it! Congratulations.

You just spent ninety days learning about the birth and early ministry of Jesus. You might feel as though you've found some answers to certain concepts about God, Jesus, and the Bible that were fuzzy for you before. Or maybe you have more questions now than when you began the journey! Both scenarios are possible, and they mean one very important thing: you have dug in and really taken this journey to heart. That is such a huge step in your Life Along the Way.

If you would like the journey to continue, pick up book two of Life Along the Way: *Jesus Among Us: Walking with Him in His Ministry and Miracles.* In that devotional, you'll learn more about the miracles and messages of Jesus— what He taught and did that changed lives.

And, just maybe, it will change your life too.

# CONTRIBUTORS TO THE LIFE ALONG THE WAY SERIES BY JOURNEYWISE

**JourneyWise** began as the passion project of Dr. Shane Stanford, a Methodist minister and author, and Dr. Ronnie Kent, a board-certified pediatrician and behavioral health specialist. These men, whose Christ-centered friendship and fellowship began nearly forty years ago, wanted to create a platform that would allow leading Christian thinkers, teachers, pastors, and content creators to share insights that would enable people to find their identity in Christ. Its faith-based media network helps people from all walks of life sit at the feet of Jesus and receive life from His Word. JourneyWise is part of The Moore-West Center for Applied Theology, which aims to train laity in biblical literacy, theological dialogue, apologetics, and critical thinking, and in serving through applied theology. It was founded for the purpose of equipping and engaging others to "love Jesus and love like Jesus" in the world. The Life Along the Way Series was developed to help fulfill that mission.

## CONTRIBUTORS:

**Dr. Shane Stanford** is the founder and CEO of The Moore-West Center for Applied Theology, as well as the president of JourneyWise, The Moore-West Center's faith-based media network. Along with pastoring congregations in Florida, North Carolina, Mississippi, and Tennessee for more than thirty years, Shane served as host of *The Methodist Hour* on TV and radio, reaching more than thirty million homes nationwide. He was awarded an honorary doctorate in divinity from Asbury Seminary, and he holds a master of divinity degree in theology and ethics from Duke University Divinity School. As an HIV-positive hemophiliac, he has spoken nationwide about AIDS awareness, including on CNN, *Good Morning America*, and Fox News. He and his wife, Pokey, have three daughters and live near Memphis.

**Dr. Ronnie Kent** recently retired after a forty-one-year practice as a medical doctor in Hattiesburg, Mississippi. He is a graduate of the University of Mississippi and the UM School of Medicine, has been teaching Bible classes in churches for decades, and is the father of three and grandfather of ten. He and his wife, Anne, have been married for forty-four years.

**Dr. Ray Cummings** has been pastoring churches for more than thirty years. A graduate of William Carey College and New Orleans Baptist Theological Seminary, he has a doctorate in ministry with a specialization in church growth and evangelism, and he is the coauthor of The 41 Series devotionals. He and his wife, Amanda, have four children and live in Purvis, Mississippi.

**Anthony Thaxton** is an Emmy Award-winning filmmaker, television producer, and painter. He directed the acclaimed documentary *Walter Anderson: The Extraordinary Life and Art of the Islander*, directed projects with Morgan Freeman and Dolly Parton, and is the producer of *Palate to Palette* on public television. His photography has been featured on *Good Morning America*, CNN, and *Fox & Friends*, and his vibrant watercolors have been featured in books and on numerous television programs. He and his wife, Amy, live in Raymond, Mississippi.

**Keelin MacGregor** is a collaborative writer, editor, and avid circus artist based in the Pacific Northwest. Coauthor of Amazon #1 new release *Jane Doe #9: A "Surviving R. Kelly" Victim Speaks Out*, covering abuse victim Lizzette Martinez, her next collaborative work, *The Deadly Path to Operation Fast and Furious*, will be coming out in spring 2024 with government whistleblower and former ATF agent Pete Forcelli.

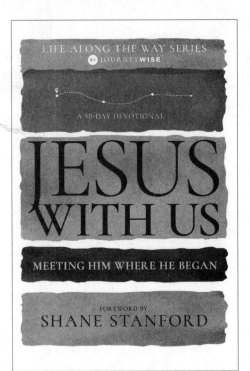

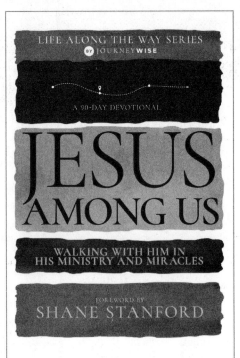

# LIFE ALONG THE WAY SERIES
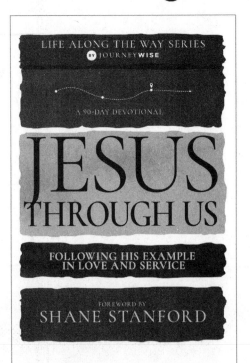

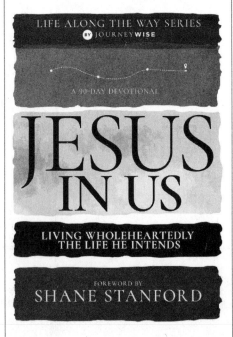